Sea of Nothing

Where Faith Works the Work of Everything

by

Scott and Jean Beemer

Sea of Nothing

Where Faith Works the Work of Everything

by

Scott and Jean Beemer

PUBLISHED IN THE UNITED STATES
by
The Tennessee Publishing House
Greeneville, Tennessee
January 2009
Sales Orders (423) 422-4711
First Edition, First Printing

Cover Design: Kelly Warren-Underwood

D i s c l a i m e r

This document is an original work of the author. It may include reference to information commonly known or freely available to the general public. Any resemblance to other published information is purely coincidental. The author has in no way attempted to use material not of his own origination. The Tennessee Publishing House disclaims any association with or responsibility for the ideas, opinions or facts as expressed by the author of this book.

Unless otherwise indicated, all scriptures are taken from the King James Version (KJ) of the Holy Bible, copyright 1970 by Thomas Nelson Inc. or from the Amplified Bible (AMP), copyright 1987 by the Zondervan Corp., and by the Lockman foundation, by permission.

**Printed in the United States of America
Cataloging-in-Publication**

ISBN: 978-1-58275-235-8
Copyright © by Scott Beemer

ALL RIGHTS RESERVED

ACKNOWLEDGEMENTS

The Holy Spirit inspired this entire book as it was received by Scott and Jean Beemer in their morning devotions.

DEDICATION

To My Bride Forever, Annetta Jean, and Scott and Susan, our son and daughter; also to our grand daughters, and grandsons and all of our great-grand daughters and all of our great grandsons all who have an intimate knowledge of and fellowship with God.

To The San Diego First Assembly of God, especially the Saints Alive Group; and to God's Open Forum.

This Book is primarily aimed and dedicated toward teaching, guiding, and loving Christians that have not yet risen to the task that Our Father has for them.

TABLE OF CONTENTS

PROLOGUE

The concept of an area that exists that is far beyond anything known to man is a concept that raises man's curiosity, or certainly should! But the glaring truth is man has already viewed it when the Hubble Space Telescope shows the edge of the known Universe as just a black wall or barrier impenetrable! Everything outside of this edge is without a doubt a real area, and it is so vast that to try to conceive of its size truly boggles the mind of any thinking man to the extent that so far there are no known reports or even interest being shown about this area.

The modern cosmologist says man has become capable of actually seeing the reality of the center to the edge of their own [The Bride of Christ's] Universe. But everything outside of this known universe is the subject of this book. In other words, man has come to the visual reality of the virtual edge of the Universe and now he is looking on the Cosmic Dark Region [So called by Cosmologists]; but God calls it His "Sea Of Nothing."

God Our Father has taken upon Himself to make a tentative report about this space calling it His "Sea Of Nothing" or S.O.N. He calls it by that name and description because there is nothing He wants to tell about it in any detail saying, man has, while in the flesh, little or no capacity to comprehend its size, scope, or its purpose. The following book explains little or nothing but the most obvious and simple explanations. This is portrayed as God's own territory, a place primarily His alone to occupy!

This story about My Sea Place is the carrot to get you to pay attention to the truths I bring to you. First you'll learn of My True

"Heaven" [The Heaven of the Heavens] and more about its size, location, and purposes. Also you'll learn about some of its gifts and wonders. You should know it is impossible to properly describe for reasons I explain later, also it is so far away from our time now that it only becomes your hope far away. I want My Bride to know that there is a place in their future far away as well as in their next coming up future. Yes your eternity will never stop opening up with magnificent wonders of all ages!

CHAPTER ONE

A Place of Slow Revelation

A DOOR OPENING

My Children your **Biblical** assignment has a far greater reach than you have imagined. Your way is most important to **The Father**, just know that all of your morning efforts of seeking in silence, listening for **My** voice, and **Bible** study are noted, and you are growing in **The Spirit.**

All time is in **God's** hands and **NOTHING** in place is out of place. Man's viewpoint is just that, the limited view from earth's place where man is seated. **The Father's** view is more than man imagines. **All of God's Universe, and beyond**, is growing in completeness, this is part of **The Father's** daily concern. Yet each child of **His** is also observed and watched over. Man's view is to be expanded as **LOVE** flows more freely. The earth will become a free flowing place of God's **LOVE EXPANDING.** *All Scripture exhibits only a tiny peek of what's unfolding before man's eyes.* The eyes of **The Spirit of God** have not yet allowed man to view the full concept of their **Heavenly** realm unfolding.

My child, rest in **Me**, lean on **Me** and all things will come together in your life. Have an attitude of Love, Peace, and Joy. Have confidence in **My Word.** *Philippians 4:10, "But My God shall supply all your need according to His riches in Glory by Christ Jesus"* Claim

My scriptures, *Philippians 4:13, "I can do all things through Christ which strengtheneth me"*. These promises are for you in your every day life. Cast about you an aura of love and peace. Be compassionate and understanding of all. Listen with patience and with a tender heart. Know that **I** am with you always; you are dwelling in **My Presence** so have confidence in that.

Ages end and new ones open. Time is but the moment's receptacle of **God's Treasures** being shown. **Do not try to imagine the vastness of Truth unfolding**, for truly **God** has layer after layer after layer of "The Leaves of Time's Pages" to set before "Man." **HIS SELF Expanding** is the act that is in process. A near place is the **NOW** a far place is the **Never Ending**, and **Time** is the pages of a **Book of No Beginnings.** Only **God's** viewpoint prevails, and total submission to it elevates man in **God's** eyes. Every child of **God** must finally come to the understanding that they are to be truly **"Like Little Children"** as the **Bible** says. This revelation accepted becomes man's final stepping stone into the reality of **His Forever** where **God** desires them to be.

Now the breakthrough begins. The Spiritual Knowledge and Understanding Is **The Blessing** in the lives of the believers, the redeemed ones. Search your **Bible, My Word**, diligently and bring forth the deeper meanings of the Scriptures. Deposit it into your heart; take it into your soul, so God can use **The Word** to expand your knowledge and understanding. Let peace like a river flood your soul, as you rest in the **Lord**, that **His** will can be completed in you. Always know **God** is good and **His** ways are the best and only way for you. Pray constantly, and then **I** may lead all the way.

Where some see Nothing apparent, the knowing ones will just know and go, following **Love's** trail of trust. **Revelation Knowledge** is **Now** to be the learning **Path of Obedience**. Do not wonder or doubt about these revelations, for Now is **Our** point of releasing new attractions to help awaken the right children of use for these last times! Just as the growing light of dawn paints the beauty of **God's** colors of the earth in slow revelation, so is **Our Father** now bringing exposure of the beauty of **His Spiritual Universe** slowly in greater reality to His children who are seeing **His Truths**. Yes dear ones this dawning of *Universal Revelation Knowledge* is the last great move being opened in theses last days of **God's Gathering Time** for the **Bride of Christ, His Son**.

Only **Truth Seekers** will see this and know through their desire becoming the **Father's** desire for them. Seek earnestly with all of your heart and soul to be chosen for these great gifts of **Truth**. Only by going through this open door will you gain your highest and best position **God** has for you in **His Eternity** of increasing wonder. Yes dear ones these next moments in the flesh time of your life are the new birth of **Grace** bringing **Divine Sufficiency** that releases you out of the bondage of the physical life. This is the **Father's Road of Release** all of **His** children must travel to find Love's open arms of forever wrapping them securely.

Acts 1:8, "And you shall receive power [ability, efficiency, and might] when the Holy Spirit has come upon you, and you shall be My witnesses in Jerusalem and all Judea and Samaria and to ends [the very bounds] of the earth." I have a place for you to work **My Will**, only when you reach that place can **We** become what the **Father** indicates in these scripture verses. When will you submit to the **Holy Spirit**?

Romans 8:29, 30, 29"For those whom He foreknew [of whom He was aware and loved beforehand]. He also destined from the beginning [foreordaining them] to be molded into the image of His Son [and share inwardly His Likeness] that He might become the first born among many brethren. 30And those whom He thus foreordained, He also called; and those whom He called, He also justified [acquitted, made righteous, putting them into right standing with Himself]. And those whom He justified, He also glorified [raising them to a heavenly dignity and condition or state of being]." Search yourself, has all this already transpired in your life? Why not? **I** am ready. **I** have been waiting for you to come to **Me**. Seek **Me** early in the morning. Seek **Me** in the silence, wait for **Me** expecting! When will you start? **I** am always there for you.

You do not have to be perfect to be used by **God**, for the best of **God's** children fall short, that's why **God's Love and Grace** must be extended to us. However **The Father** can't use you in great power if you do not flow in the stream of **His Love,** surrendered to **His will**.

Matthew 8:11, "I tell you, many will come from east and west, and will sit at table with Abraham, Issac, and Jacob in the Kingdom of Heaven." This scripture refers to you as you put yourself in **My Hands**!

However, **God** cannot move in great power unless a great number of **His** children are surrendered to **His Will and Way** in these very last days of "**The Gathering**." They are to find no path but just the path of obedience to the words **The Father** brings. Only by obedience, with understanding, can man accomplish the things put before him. *Sow the ideas and words put in your heart* and you will reap the harvest of the **Universe** in all of its potential and fullness. Hear **My Word** to you this day, and find no delay or hesitation in our compliance.

My children, as much as is possible, every day live in the **Spirit**. The physical or worldly things will take care of themselves. Be in the **Spirit**, walking with **Me**, as you do the worldly things **I** have put before you! By putting all things in **My Hands** they will be accomplished with ease. Do all things as unto **The Lord** and life will be a joy. Keep your mind on Christ, your thoughts pure, and your words positive and of good report. Remember always *"Greater is He that is in you than he that is in the world."* Rely on the power of **God**, and the **Holy Spirit**, to lead the way and be your strength.

In searching **My Word** the worthy reader, seeking **My Truth**, will find much more than that; for **I** will pull the plug that withholds and release **Kingdom Wealth** in abundance. He that reads **My Words**, holding them up for close scrutiny, will find much more than new thinking, for **I** will release hidden truths leading to new plateaus of Love and excitement. These seekers are the ones that **I** look for to bless more abundantly. It will be wise for them to draw ever closer to **Me** each day, not week by week, but day by day until days blend as one into the great evermore.

Question all **I** say with a strong desire to know only what's true, and **I** will turn on the light of everlasting **LOVE**. For all truth exposes all **LOVE** that never will end! **My** dear ones there is one great prize that never will die, the desire for **Ever Increasing Knowledge**. This is the end to never be found *for I AM that end!* There are many great forces at work in the world today, but none are as strong and as powerful as the force you know and work with! Keep drawing closer, and you will know, and be made well aware of the things here implied!

Today **I** would have you rest in **The Lord**. Let self rest and allow the **Holy Spirit** to lead the way. Let the **Holy Spirit** develop you faith, and give you more peace and joy, and strengthen your trust in **God**! Everything becomes less difficult when you are working in **My Presence**, doing it **My Way**. See things in a new light, the light that **I** bring. It will dispel darkness and wrong thinking. Open your mind to **Me**; allow **My Presence** to dominate your thinking and feelings. Release the **Holy Spirit** to bring blessings into your life.

Make your desires **My** desires and **Our** desires will prevail. Do not discontinue your searching in **My Word**, for that is fodder for **My** work. Only **Heart's Desire** works with **Me**. **Man's** heart is My plowed and planted field to grow **My** hopes and purposes. Only **My** Listening Ones are tools for **My** plans and purposes to be shown. This world is not "man's" toy to run. Only **My** Children who Listen, Hear, and Obey will emerge as victors on the stages of this world. Have no doubts, **I Am The Master of Time**, and **I** will set the stage of success!

Always keep My Will and Way
Doing the things I Say

*********PAY ATTENTION*********

When the cares of this world close in on you then you should sit down and seek Me in the quiet time. Our Time is to be your time of silent growth in the **Spirit**. Turn your attention to **Spirit Time** with **Me**. You are to draw from **Our Time** a new strength and confidence in Our growing bond of **Love**. Yes, **Spirit** growth in love is **My** children's answer to their earth-flesh problems, but few know how to draw benefit from **Our Oneness. You and I have a bonding in the Spirit realm that needs serious attention!** Part of your needed growth only comes when you give **Me** free time with you. **Our** bonding takes time because the earth-flesh is slow to work with, and **We** don't have proper time together.

My child, **I** have drawn you to **Me** that you would be **My** beloved child of **God**, part of the Family of **God**, the **Bride of Christ**. Go through this time on earth, this testing and growing time, in faith that **I** am with you. Forget the things that are behind, and push forward to the things ahead. Walk always in **Love, in Peace and Joy**. Always walk in **My Presence** and in **My Glory** so that **I** may use you to show **My Love and Peace** to others. Trust that your prayers are being heard. **I** am working for your good. You are to grow Spiritually and humble yourself, so **I** can lead you on the path **I** have prepared for you. Do your part, so **I** can do more. Step out in Faith.

TRUTH SEEKERS

Search for and seek out **Truth Seekers** for they are the bedrock of **My Family**. Never forsake **My TRUTH**. It flows as a river, or sometimes as a waterfall, before **My Loved Ones. My Time** of washing is close, so very close, and is now for all who hunger and seek for **My True Ways**. Rewards, yes great are **My** rewards for all **Truth Seekers.** Feed those who seek, fill their hunger, for they are the ones who will grow and flourish in **My Will and Way**. There is no end in sight for those who are truly fed and filled with **My Truths** for they will never hunger or hurt again.

My Path never diminishes or leads anyone astray; only the first peek at **My Truths** inspires and sets true hearts on fire for more! Always broadening, expanding, and increasing is **My Way in Truth**. Always broader, deeper, and more vast than ever imagined is the way of **My Truth. The Heavens** can't contain it, there is not room enough in **The Universe** so ever-growing is **My Truth**. Only **My Love** is greater and more to be desired. Only **Love** leads all **Truth Seekers.**

No **Truth Seeker** ever goes far without **Love Leading** all the time! **My Love** is the Forever Foundation of all **I Am**. Earth is but a primitive display of **Love and Truth**, for like fields of forever **My Truth** and **Love** wave as stalks of corn and waves of wheat. They stretch out before **My** children as far as the eyes of their imaginations can see! **I** give revelation knowledge to the "**True Truth Seekers**" only! These are the times to stir the waters so the **True Truth Seekers** will clearly see. Know **My Ways** of sure victory.

FIRST PLACE OF NOTHING

A SEARCH INTO NOTHING'S PLACE
TO OPEN REALITY IN NEW WAYS.

My S.O.N. [Sea of Nothing] is all encompassing in that it is everywhere all of the time; nothing exists that is outside of **My Sea**. Yes its size is beyond all comprehension of man. Yes it carries all things that ever was or ever will be. Yes man can not see, feel, understand or even know the size, intensity, frequency, or force of it. There exists nothing outside of it for it has no inside, outside or round about! It is more than that! Why do **I** wish to talk about this? Because soon **My Family** will know where **I Am**, and all that **I Am. Am I** not their **Father**?

I am expressing **My Presence** through **My Family**; all of this is **My Desire. I** am making this Family so **Love** will grow and grow and **expand Love** by giving more of **Me** for **Love** to enjoy. As is, "**I Am**," so is **My S.O.N. My** dear children have a right of entrance reaching into **My Place**. It is what **I** desire to give them [an inheritance] therefore **I** must start their education sometime, some where, *so I begin!* Until all are in the **Spirit I** *cannot show or do too much, but some sort of entry must begin, so here We are starting!*

Is not all of this understandable from man's standpoint? What truly is **Jesus'** inheritance? **Does any man know**? Yes, **I've** opened man's soul and **Spirit** to seek and see more of the **Universe** than has ever been told. Many children are now coming into agreement about many new things in the **Heavens**, but I've only cracked the door a little for what they are seeing. When **I** gather the **Bride** [Church] then this ongoing revelation of Heaven will become a base to extend all **I'm** now showing to man.

Can you see some reasonableness about all of this? **I'm** looking for men of **Mine** who have a listening ear and a ready comprehension without useless questioning and doubts! Fear is so ready to turn man from this sort of thing, but fear is evidence of uselessness to **Me**! **I** am keeping this simple for now, as **I've** said, **I** need some-place sure to start!

A LOOK AT OUR FOUNDATION

The Bible is **Our** only sure foundation so let's take a look at some interesting scriptures: [From the *King James* or the *Amplified Bibles*]

Mark 8:17-21, 17"And when Jesus knew it, he saith unto them, why reason ye, because ye have no bread? Perceive ye not yet, neither understand? Have ye your heart yet hardened? 18Having eyes, see ye not? And having ears, hear ye not? And do ye not remember? 19When I brake the five loaves among five thousand, how many baskets full of fragments took ye up? They say unto him twelve. 20And when the seven among the four thousand, how many baskets full of fragments took ye up? And they said, seven. 21And he said unto them, how is it that ye do not understand?" Now these scriptures *are doing one thing and that is they question the understaning of the disciples.* Ask yourselves these same questions about your understanding about this subject **We** are displaying. Is not **The Father** fully able to accomplish all that is being put before you? Study the following scriptures seeking **The Truth** of all that is being released.

Hebrews 11:1-3, 1"Now faith is the substance of things hoped for, the evidence of things not seen. 2For by it the elders obtained a good report. 3Through faith we understand that the worlds were framed by the word of God, so that things which are seen were not made of things which do appear." This scripture is speaking to you directly about your walk in the **Spirit** with **Me**. Do you move in and with the **Holy Spirit**? Are you moving in **Revelation Knowledge** and being obedient to **My** voice daily? *II Corinthians 5:7, "For we walk by faith [we regulate our lives and conduct our-selves by our conviction or belief respecting man's relationship to God and divine things, with trust and holy fervor; thus we walk]." not by sight or appearance.* Is your walk daily led by the **Lord**? Do you do **His** will daily as **He** asks you to? Are you in daily con-verse with **Him**?

II Corinthians 4:18, "Since we consider and look not to the things that are seen but to the things that are unseen; for the things that are visible are temporal [brief and fleeting], but the things that are invisible are deathless and everlasting." Are you led daily by the **Holy Spirit**? Do you enter into this tale of **Nothing** understanding the things **I'm** speaking of here, at least somewhat? *Romans 8:25, "But if we hope for that we see not, then do we with patience wait for it."* How is your patience with the things I tell that are on **My Heart**? Do you wait upon **Me** morning by morning, seeking My voice of guidance?

Romans 4:1,. "As it is written, I have made you a father of many nations. [He was appointed our father] in the sight of God in whom he believed, Who gives life to the dead and speaks of the nonexist-ent things that [He has foretold and promised] as if they already existed." Are We in touch each morning speaking one to another? Are you understanding what **I'm** relating to you here?

Mark 11:22-24, 22"And Jesus answering saith unto them, Have faith in God. 23For verily I say unto you, That whosoever shall say unto this mountain, Be thou removed, and be thou cast into the sea; and shall not doubt in his heart, but shall believe that those things which he saith shall come to pass; he shall have whatsoever he saith 24Therefore I say unto you, What things soever ye desire, when ye pray, believe that ye receive them, and ye shall have them." Are you daily walking in obedience to this kind of word **I** give you? Why not? Do you receive what you ask for through **Me**? *Isaiah 46:10, "Declaring the end from the beginning, and from ancient times the things that are not yet done, saying, My counsel shall stand, and I will do all my pleasure."* This scripture is stating that which **I** am presenting to you now. Yes **I** am declaring things for the end of the **Church Age**. It is **My Pleasure** to open to you the things you should learn to receive and believe helping you in these times to be better prepared for your place with **Me** that is just ahead for you.

Isaiah 42:9, "Behold, the former things are come to pass, and new things do I declare: before they spring forth I tell you of them." **Today you are reading the new things** that are about to come to pass. **I** am opening the eyes of those who listen and hear **Me** early in the morning.

GOD'S HELP

TAKE SPIRIT'S EAR IN YOUR HEART,
MAKE GOD'S VOICE CLEAR FROM THE START.
I'LL LEAD YOUR WAY SO YOU'LL KNOW
IT'S ONLY MY WILL YOU SHOULD SHOW.

BY OBEDIENCE MY CHILDREN GROW
IN WAYS I DESIRE THEY SHOULD GO.
SO LISTEN WELL AND THEN OBEY,
I'LL COME INTO YOUR HEART TODAY.

BLESS MY HEART WITH SONGS TO SING
KEEP THE TUNE THAT LOVE WILL BRING.
BY KNOWING IT WELL THEN ALL MAY SAY
THIS MAKES OUR GOD-FILLED DAY.

BLENDING LIVES WITH GOD FILLED LOVE,
START EACH DAY WITH POWER FROM ABOVE.
IT'S SENT TO THE CHILDREN, ALL BELIEVERS,
WHO WITH GOD'S HELP BECOME ACHIEVERS.

CHAPTER TWO

More of Sea of Nothing

To keep on the search of **Nothing's Place I** will open reality in new ways. Yes you are coming into a place of discovery that hides much more than ALL **I've** ever told about **My Real Place of Everlasting Dwelling**. You are making progress into the unseen, that's the **Place of Nothing, only Spirit teaching brings one to Spirit's Place**. Where better to hide **My** doings of **Future, Present, and the Past** than in the place of **Great Nothing**. Why do **I** call it nothing? Because "No Thing" about it has ever been revealed. Remember, **I** teach you to look at things that are not [that is nothing] as if they were! This today is not silly "nothing" confusion but simply insight into thinking that opens up to **My Places of Great Wonder. The Universe is expanding into My Sea of Nothing**, a place never mentioned by man, But where else could this expansion be going?

Yes, **My** child **I** have also given you the authority over evil. Use this authority daily. Have faith that **My Word** is **True**. *"Submit yourself unto God. Resist the devil and he will flee from you."* Use the power over the devil you have been given. Receive the freedom in the **Lord** that is available to you. Don't allow evil to spoil your walk with **God**. Be the over-comer that **God** created you to be. Take dominion over evil around you so that you may be free to experience the presence and **Love of GOD**.

The **Sea Of Nothing** is filled with **Me** and **My Things**. No man can ever understand, but **I** speak to all men as if they are **One** [in **Spirit** with Me]. In **My S.O.N. Faith** works the works of everything and no man knows. Here is the **Work Room of Forever**, and everything exists that is, is to be, or has been. Believing is man's doorway, and **Faith** is the path to **Forever**. **Time** is laid out showing where ALL can be, and No "man" walks to trails where **Nothing** leads, and all things are hidden where **Forever** unfolds. Seeing is not, because **I AM** the **Great "SEE"** of **ALL**. Waiting is stretching **Time** out of **Nothing**, and **Time** crumbles at the speed of **Time**. All "Light" is **Forever** and **My Children** follow **Light**. Knowing only opens the doorway where no "man" enters, but **My** children have left manhood for **Me**. This is a tale from **Nothing** where no "man" sees, but **ALL My Children** will know!

Rise up and know that **I Am God. I Am your God**, you are **My** beloved child. Cast your cares upon **Me** for **I** care for you. Rest in **Me** always. Wait upon **Me** to have your strength renewed. Let **My** peace come upon you and sustain you in harmony, then the joy will follow. Be not anxious for all is well [Say all is well *all of the time*], **My Time** is the right time. Go forward filled with joy. Walk in **My** presence and fill your being with **Jesus**. This will eliminate self and the worldly ways in your life. Be filled with **My Love** and **Glory**, then go forth sharing with others the **Love of the Lord**!

PAUSE FOR CONTEMPLATION

The days are fast fleeing, and then this time will end, and suddenly a new birth of wonder unfolds. How few men are occupied in this unknown, as yet, "**Wonder**." Never be found not caring and not sharing these truths here given. If you do no more than tell a friend it becomes a break in your dam of self trust and belief! **All, all the children of God, must reach awareness of My everlasting presence**. Let this come about by spending time in silence in **My Presence**! It is your growth building when you seek more and more of **My Plan** for you, but it is **My "Joy"** you are restraining and holding back when your disobedience flourishes!

Come grow and flower more and more as self is left by the wayside. **Our** coming together is not some time in the future, but has already been accomplished. Every child of **Mine** should be living and walking in this belief. **There is no great happening in the future that is greater than that which already happened at your time of new birth and at your water baptism**! **My** dear one live each day as if **Our Oneness** were already accomplished, for it is, it has been done, there is no greater time ahead. If you understand, and believe, and **live now** as if all is done, then **Our** walk and talk with **Me** is **Our** living in **Our Oneness**.

Take this that **I** say to you daily as of no more importance than what you have already confessed before, that you are a child of the living **God**. If **I** believed that then, and you believed that then, then why would there ever be any doubt that it is true? Learn to live today as you will be living every day with **Me** in the future. Come as you make **Our Love** real, "**Now**," and you can know **Our Love's reality of Forever**!

I have given you **the authority to rule over the power of darkness. We** are **One, I Am the Head** and you are the body. **We** act as **One**. When **Jesus** was raised from the dead **you were raised with Him**. You have the "**Resurrection Power**." Take a stand against evil, cast it out in the **Name of Jesus**. Plead **Jesus'** cleansing blood over the objects of your prayers and know that **God's** power is working in their lives. *"There is power in the blood of the Lamb."* Use the authority you have been given as a believer!

**Make this day a GREAT TURNING POINT in
your heart.**
*******7-7-07*******
**Yes make this day one you will always
Remember.**

BECAUSE WITH ME IT IS A
"CENTER POINT"
OF ALL MY PLANS IN THE
LIFE OF FOREVER.

*"Thy word is a lamp unto my feet, and a light unto my path." Ps. 119:105. AMP_***My Word** is your written record of what **I** desire you to begin to understand, but **My Word that I speak to you** is truly the light to your personal path **I** expect you to follow. Only through **My Word** to you will you ever grow where you should!

"Arise, shine; for thy light has come, and the Glory of the Lord is risen upon thee." Isaiah 60:1. **DO YOU BELIEVE**? Take this personally and walk in it daily, listening until **We** have **Our** true place to walk in love! Until **We** become personally acquainted you will not have **My Light** shinning on your path!

Watch, Listen, and Learn how the winds of advantage and adversity collide. **My** hand guides and watches over all. **ALL**. Never believe the things you see and hear as if that were the **ALL** of everything, **Truth** releases only **My Will and Way** whether good or bad as judged by man. **My** children judge not! Learn to trust and wait upon **Me**.

MORE OF NOTHING

Our ongoing walk must grow in this **NO THING** place because in the unseen **I** can bring new truth to obedient listeners who are beeing prepared in the **Spirit** to be led as if **I** were with them always. When this "as if" is made a walking, waking reality all of the time, then their obedience will be assured! **I'm** drawing **My** lines of separation and only the **Truth Seekers**, seeking **My Truths**, will find their way. Only **My Way** leads to truth which is your victory! Use your tools of escape wisely; **My Bible, My Holy Spirit, My Son**, and **My Love**! Hear **My Voice**, obey **My Call**, and know this way each day is the only way. Draw **My** lost ones with you, telling them **I'm** coming soon! Close not your ears lest your heart withers away!

My child, keep your eyes on **My Son Jesus**. The enemy is about you, use your authority as a child of God. Remember **My Word** *"Submit yourself unto God, resist the devil and he will flee from thee."* Do not allow him to secure a place in your life. Walk always in **My Presence**. Have faith that **I Am** with you. Plead the blood of **My Son** over yourself, your family, your house, car, and over those you love. Believe there truly is power in the blood, Let **My Word** have a place in your heart and soul. Be led by the **Truth** in **My Word**, and the **Holy Spirit I** have given you. Walk uprightly in love and peace. Let no evil be in your life. Take and use the authority **I** have given to you. **We** are **One in Spirit, My Power** is your power. **Walk** in this knowledge.

Now today is given to those with ears to hear and heads to see and understand, and hearts that carry **My Truth** to know and do the work I call for. Seek to know **My Will and Way**! No man is exempt from all that is being written. See now the great need to tell **My Lost Ones** about these times they are in? Just think as you look about you, these are some of the people that will be living through all the horror of the **tribulation**!

When **I** cause a thing to come about **I** will never stop halfway, but man is and has been a most trying, testing endeavor! **Our Family** is and will be a very interesting desire of **Mine. I** tell them of promises of unbelievable beauty and wonder, and they seem to dismiss the reality of it all and wander in their own dream. This should not be! Come dear ones **and seek only My purposes, My desires, and My Plans.**

I assure you **I** truly know what's for your **Best**! All paths of mankind do not lead to any place **I've** prepared for them; wake up to this reality in your future. **My Wonders in Forever** man can't ever imagine! Follow **My** guidance as **I** direct your path, and do as **Jesus** did, "**Do nothing except what I tell you or show you**." Follow **My** lead daily and learn to put your feet where **I** direct, and then heaven will open to show you **My Wonders of Forever**! Tell **My** children their time of choosing is fast disappearing!

GIVE UP SIN

HERE COMES THE SUN, SOON IT'S NOON, DAY TURNS NIGHT.

A CYCLE ENDLESS FOR MAN TO SEEK AND FIND WHAT'S RIGHT.

OKAY FOR YOU, WRONG FOR A FEW, DOES DAY BRING SIGHT?

WHETHER DARKNESS OR IF IT'S DAWN ALL NEED THE LIGHT.

JESUS IS THE WAY NO MAN LOST, TRY WITH ALL YOUR MIGHT!

DRAW JESUS IN, GIVE UP SIN, YOU WILL WIN THE FIGHT.

CHAPTER THREE

My Great Sea [S.O.N.]

Just knowing about **My GREAT SEA [My S.O.N.]** sets you in a rare place of knowing! There are so many things in **My Great Sea**; this subject carries the all of everything that ever was and ever will be. No one knows but **I** know, no one cares, but **I** care. Still this vastness can't hold all **I** have. Only **My Son** carries the key and only **My Spirit** and **Jesus** know **Me** and **Mine**. This **Sea** is not **My Families**, only **My Universe** is theirs. Soon this breakthrough will show, and then will begin the **Era of Ages**. Preparations take time and time covers **Ages**.

Now all of this is just before **My Family**. This spread of preparation covers **Love and Joy** growing as **The Great Banquet** of all forever is being readied. **My** children grow as **Love** spreads peace, pleasure, and joy of life. All this will build in **My Universe of Growing. Space** is only a place, and growing is only **Me** in **Expansion**. There will never be others only **Me**. **I AM** all that ever will be, and all of **Us** are just **Me. We are One** and **One** is only **I AM!**

MY WORD

My child, rise up and do for others around you. Be generous to those doing **My** work. Be the loving **Spirit I** have created you to be. Do receive **My** peace, and let all blessings flow. **Listen, be still and know that I am God. I Am** building you up, preparing you for the time ahead. *"I can do all things through Christ which strengthens me."* Trust this Word, **My Word** is true and everlasting. It has been given to and for **My Children**. So deposit it into your heart [Spirit] and soul that you may be strengthened and enlightened.

In the raising up of a child to become a useful servant in **My Kingdom** many steps must be taken. Teaching, training, testing, and tellin, all of these at the opportune time must fit into **My Plan,** and bring many together that **all may be as One in Purpose**! This only works when complete trust and obedience has been attained. The difficulty is obvious, none **I** pick is perfect because of free will. Attention holding becomes a problem because of the enemy and the self involved. **My Plan** of first sending the **Holy Spirit**, then **Jesus** into each child is the final, and only safe way, to bring the **Oneness Principal** into each child before **I** make the finalization with **My Indwelling** each one. This is the safe-guard only **I** can give to assure the everlasting safety of **My Sea Of Nothing**!

MY SEA

This is a simple story of **My Way** to increase **My Love** more and more. This just said is the only overall picture **I** have ever given about **My Sea**! This is to furnish a written record of **My** total desire, and it is so no deviation will come about. There is no end, and there is no other purpose than **This is as I desire**. The far flung activities are to insure all things are going to flow in an orderly way, and no time ever interferes with this unfolding. **I** tell all of this so those **I** love will have this comfort of knowing **My Plan and Purposes** have great and exciting times ahead. One thousand years are given for setting everyone in their proper place for their secure future in the **Earth** and **Universe**. These are the stages set for the first generation in **My** new expansion, and all this is but a fresh start into **My Sea Of Nothing** where all **My** things are.

Hebrews 1:2, "[But] in the last days He has spoken to us in [the person of a] Son. Whom He appointed Heir and lawful Owner of all things, also by and through Whom He created the worlds and the reaches of space and the ages of time [He made, produced, built, operated, and arranged them in order]."

This recording of **Nothing** has set **Nothing** on the stage of something, somewhere. This is a breakthrough so big that it is truly a **Doorway of Love** making the exposure of **Nothing** into something. This **First Time Move** is going along the **Father's** path of exposure into a realm of new reality. The breakthrough is like a fine sized hole in a great dam drawing the unknown into a new life of change. **My way grows with change's exposure making new out of Nothing.** This is bringing a wind of growing worth, allowing man's return from his **Creation Place**. Change is **Love** expanding; **Love** expanding becomes the **Father's Outreach** exposing **His Realm of Joy's Increase**.

LOVE'S WONDERS

All of this releasing is a new way! Yes, this is **Right** coming to its own newness. **The Father** knows all of **His Things** in **His Ocean of Nothing** must come to this time of flexing that will produce a new time for **Eternities** change. **The Earth and Universe are coming into their planned place for the Ages now set to open**. All this is no wild uncontrolled release, but **ALL** is under very careful watch. **God's** children will have their time to experience **Love's Wonder's** in **Fullness of Joy**. All of this just ahead is making **God's Growth** [in **His** Children] assured just as **His Plan** desired for **Him**.

This is a time of division. Both good and evil have been loosed in this world. It is a time of decision, of choosing which way each man will go. **I** tell you to *"Arise, shine, for thy light is come, and the glory of the Lord is risen upon thee."* The darkness around about you is not for you. You are a **Child of Light**, a **Child** of **My Love and Glory**. Claim what **I** have for you and **walk** in **My Love**, in **My Light** always.

To **Help** you understand "Non-existent things" read the following scriptures; II Corinthians 4:18, *"While we look not at the things which are seen, but at the things which are not seen: for the things which are seen are temporal; but the things which are not seen are eternal."* As We view the earth and people around us, all that our eyes are viewing are just temporal! Also all that you are not seeing is **My S.O.N.**

Again, **Romans 4:17**, *"[As it is written I have made thee a father of many nations], before him whom he believed, even God, who quickeneth the dead. And calleth those things which be not as though they were."* Give this intense scrutiny until light dawns!

II Corinthians 5:7, "Therefore if any man be in Christ, he is a new creature: old things are passed away; behold, all things are become new" If you walk in this **truth** it is not by sight! *Hebrews 11:3, "Through faith we understand that the worlds were framed by the word of God, so that things which are seen were not made of things which do appear."* Is it possible for you to have some understanding of **My S.O.N.** now?

MY PLACE

Things invisible are deathless and everlasting like God's Sea of Nothing. This work of **Ours** is building into the place the **Father** wants. Only by drawing closer each day will this continue. Yes there is a climax! Yes, there is a **Blessing**! Yes there is a door opening, but Only when you say yes to all that is being asked of you. No guessing, no wondering, will bring more, only obeying, believing, and achieving will be all that is to be opened for these last days. Consecration, dedication and submission are the only pathways to apprehending!

Yes, this that **I** have opened up about **My Place** is to be brought more into prominence and you are the ones the **Father** has opened up to this revelation. This is very important, and this is to become more important to the **Bride's** future. Only slow revelation is to be the way. **For now is the slow, hard to walk path of opening revelation**. The things **I** desire will be released. **I** break the hold **I've** put upon your plans and there will flow more and more from **My Place of Nothing.**

MY FAMILY

"The Joy of the Lord is My strength." Maintain a **Spirit of Joy** and contentment, let peace flood your soul. Always trust the **Lord** has **His** hand on you, and **He** is lifing you up. Enjoy your fellowship with the **Lord**, and trust **Him** to lead you through all situations. Pray and keep loved ones being healed, restored, and drawing closer to **God. Thank Him** for answering your prayers. Let faith rise up, and know **God** hears you, and **He** is answering your prayers. You and your family are **My Family**, the **Bride of Christ** and **My Loved Ones**. Rest in **Me** and walk always in **Love!**

There are new changes, and growth flooding and filling these end time plans and desires. Victory will not wait on healings, miracles, and things of finished Grace. As this breaks forth **My** children will sense this change. Cooperation and agreement will work **My Work** of growing **Grace**. Let **My Love** find more room in all you do, look on each one as growing true and new, and by singing songs of heartfelt **love** receive growing awareness of this new release from above. Let new things freely enter, let pleasant times be free. Yes, have a growing knowing of your walk with **Me** in new powers of expression, new words and ways of love. Know **We** are sensing growth from this release of **Love!**

You are **My child**, you have been redeemed. You do not do works to be saved, but because you are **Mine** and you love **Me**! The works that you do should be the ones **I** have asked of you. The works you do should be out of **Love** one for another. Fill your heart with thoughts of **Jesus** and there will be no room left for self! **Love** one another as **I** have loved you. Let the fruit of the **Spirit** be manifested in your life every day. Release self to do the bidding of the **Holy Spirit**. You are able because what **He** asks you to do **He** will strengthen you and make you able. Go in peace, resting in **Me**!

MY WAY

Things of worth come not from man, only what **I** give has proven worth. As **I** share and tell of **My Way I** give directions by what **I** say. Where else will such **truth** flow telling man where and how to go? Let all of this fly away undone and not releasing day by day, then the loss, who knows the cost? Only listening and obeying **Me** now will ever prove just how man should gather **Nothing** when he doesn't sow.

If Nothing is done day by day this then is not **The Nothing** on **My Plan**. All **My Nothing** is what man may come to know, but man's nothing leaves nothing to show. Come build with **Me** but it may be **Nothing** man can see. Understand the places **I** plan are far away, but close some day. To learn now before all else is shown should bring blessings slowly grown. Try to be open when no openings shows. **My Truth** is hidden, **My Truth** little known, but over time much can be shown. All earth's places, times, and things never seem to be the great depth of truth **My** things will bring. This writing carries much, but all that's hidden carries more. Only drawing close as you can will be the way for growing man.

Filling space is like building book cases for knowledge desired, but not allowing light to see. There is a time for man to see, but for now it's not to be. Why would **I** save and hide treasure grown if worth to man was never shown? Man must grow in **Spirit** and time for all **I** plan for Him to view. Just take this personally before you are allowed to see. If now some **truth** were to be known only to a few could it be shown. Things worthwhile have meanings to few, before or until its time for all to view. Trust is for man, but for now must be a block and a barrier to the **Nothing of Me**. This peek is just for a few to view, for its worth is without estimate no price, no clue. The **Nothing I** hold is so great the words fail to show **My Estate!** So if no words could a picture paint what is **My** choice but to sit and wait!

My Truth

Each day has a price, and to view and know, the price must be paid. Close attention is time spent, but to carry the worth of each day means knowing is growing, and remembering this can bring all the victory into one event. How can **I** spread knowledge without letting time pass? If **My** children do not listen, hear and learn to do, then loss is all they can gather. All time has great worth in action, but action without **My Direction** causes losses of great worth. How can worthlessness be shown? Just by viewing Nothing grown. The Nothing of man has been scattered since time began, and all **My Beauty** and **My Gifts** wasteaway. So wake up and ride my way, then time will be spent making a new day. Do not lay around wasting what has just been found, only time spent in **My Time and Care** will ever bring success for all to share.

I have given you **My Name**, The **Word of God**, and the **Father** has sent the **Holy Spirit** to indwell you and be your comforter and helper! Remember all these blessings and use them, call upon them daily. In prayer, pray in **My Name** and all things you ask for, believing, you shall have. Never waver in your faith. Have as your moral compass **The Word of God**. Keep your eyes on **Me** [**Jesus**] for truly **I am the Way, the Truth and the Life**, and no man shall come to the **Father** but through **Me!** Lift **Me** up and **I** will draw all men unto **Me! Our** time is developing something new; be more pleased with what you do. **I** know your interest in future things and all the knowledge that **I** bring. Slow release of knowledge is given, drawing **My Children** into their new place for living. Oh there are so many places and things to be shown, riches displayed, and beauty grown. All **Heaven** is excited, but finding the future is so slow in coming. Yes there is an eagerness growing in all **My Places** as this age is summing.

THERE'S AN US

The works of men will always be strange to **My Believers**, but know this, only hearts pure and simple will finally be chosen. Study only the things **I** show you, then **I** will know you are **Mine**! Draw closer to **Me**, and don't depend as much on what you see, or begin to believe, or by what you achieve. Learn to listen with a true desire, then **We** can come together for the things **I** inspire! Make your day about **Me**, then **I'll** teach you what you should be! **Listen** and **Hear** is important each day! Left alone man tends to stray. Even in **My Word** man roams about, when he's not heard he's leaving **Me** out. Read and study but come to **Me**, for only by revelation knowledge can **I** keep the feet of man on the way that **I** Plan. Until **There's an US** there's always a fuss!

When **My** call goes out to anyone, **I** expect their attention! **I** do not waste **My Time** with hesitating doubters. Pick up what **I** am saying and find your place in this that **We** are doing. **Keep only focused on My Now with you**, not on anything past. The past is only a place of what was, you should be seeking **always to be in the Now with Me**! Yes, the present is **My Time** and **My Place** and must become yours also. Together **Our Walk** grows and develops into what must take place! Togetherness is the only walk of true growth. Seek always **True Growth**. This is the "Lesson Most Necessary" to be taught to all of **My** dear ones. Yes, "All," no matter who they think they are or how they believe, should grow fulfilling, not their own private desires, but **Mine** only.

In the long run of earth things it is still **My Will** and **My Will** only that each one will have to be obedient to. **Come each and every-one, give up self and self-pleasing, that is the loser's path of diminshing. I'm** talking like this because **truth** is the only way of walking for all of **My** children, yet many can not give release to **Me** as they should. None of this talk has anything to do with anyone losing their salvation, but is has everything to do with their final place and eternal position with **Me! Keep My Word!**

Open your mind to **The Words of the Scriptures**. They were given to you, **My** children, for your instruction, and for encouragement, to be your guide in life. Be ye lifted up and be doers of **My Word**. Be led by **My Holy Spirit**, and you will know all **truth**. Receive whole heartedly the blessings **I** have for you through the **Holy Spirit**. Live a life of love, peace, and joy, having patience with all men. See the goodness in others, and let your faith be expanded as you grow closer to the **Lord. The Holy Spirit** within you is **the voice of your Lord and Savior**. Hear what **He** is saying to you!

MY NOW

Only obedience counts in these final days. Such a future, such an end to such a beautiful plan of **Jesus** and the **Father**, only by **His** great **Love** does all of this human wonder unfold on time and on schedule. No matter man's foot dragging over the years, **The Father** has never hesitated or turned from **His** original intent. The continued unfolding of man's role shows **God's Hand** guiding all things. Yes, all of this unknown [by man] growth will finally progress into **My Nothing**. [You and **I** know now what that means, don't **We?**]

In the Glory of the Lord is peace, joy, and love. Walk in **His Glory** daily and allow the **Lord** to use you. **He** is preparing you to go to the next level of **Glory!** Enjoy life each day as you are being led in your **Spiritual** journey by the **Holy Spirit**. Always keep your eyes on **Jesus** and have the mind of **Christ**, and trust that the **Holy Spirit** will lead the way. I will lift you up and renew your strength, and when you are weak **I** am strong. Do, *"Cast all your care upon Me, for I care for you."* Be ye renewed in power and wisdom for you are **My** children!

This is the proper approach for all of **My** dear ones to come to **Me**, "Morning, Noon or Night." When **I** am put in the place of "Always" in their hearts then **My Now** is open for them to enter. **"Now"** is seldom or never spoken about, but **it is the true place of My Abode**. From **Now** is to see forward, backward, and all about! **"All About" is another name for My Sea of Nothing**—-can't you understand where **Now** is? Why bring these things up to you? Because **I** have opened **My "Sea"** to you, and now **I** desire to explain more of **My** whole position.

Nowhere has this much been shown; and this release is **My Desire at** this time; **I** require a record of all this! The whole and final **Why** is of no consequence at this time. This is only as **I desire to please Me**. Why, why, why, always man seeks into everything because they are **My Children** growing as **I** desire them to. Man sees time as ever ongoing, and there is some truth to that, but **Ongoing** and **Always** are much more to **Me**. There is no easy way to show to man, in the flesh, these things, Places, Ways, Future, Past, all about the "Heavens," Macro, and Micro worlds etc.

You see all of this is **My NOW** at once and no one can yet grasp all of that! All of this **NOW** [Sea of Nothing, Universe, Heavens, Earth, and more yet untold] will become a growing place throughout the future of **My Children**. There will be their places of inquiry, and the things of their future. **I want them to have somewhere, sometime more exposure to what is meant in My Bible when it is written they are Heirs to all I have!** And **I** will open some of this up in **My** chapter on **Heavens**. In this writing here should be exposed some kind of a better picture of their future. They should be convinced that **I** have a few things to keep them occupied over time!

MY LOVE

Rise up and know that you are a child of **God**. Walk accordingly, in peace, humbly following the will of **God**. Remember **My Words**, *"My God shall supply all your needs according to His riches in Glory by Christ Jesus."* Your daily needs are being met so walk boldly forward. Go forth in **My Love and Peace**. Be a beacon of **My Love and Compassion**. Let the **Word of God** be your covering. Claim all the promises in the scriptures for yourself and **I** will lift you up.

These notes keep opening up to things on **My Heart** for all of **My** dear ones. These notes are meant to bring you enough proof and knowledge that those who do open up to the things exposed here will have **Truth**, in reality, that they will find continual blessings day by day. To explore **My Ways** and **Places** should cause such **True Believing** in the hearts and minds of each one so exposed that teaching should become their most eager desire. Put simply they will be so filled with the wonder of **My Truths** they can't help but tell others! Oh how **I** wish more dear ones would open up to this stream of information of **Mine**. **I** hold back nothing when **I** have the proper audience! To hear with their ears the sounds of this world can take a good piece of Forever, **but to learn to hear with their Spirit's ears is to fill their Forever with ALL WAYS.**

I have not yet opened up to those growing in the flesh much of **All** that **I** am telling about in these writings, but the **Church** is on the brink of disclosure into the **Spirit Realm of My Reality** and these things here told are only to instruct and encourage the **LISTEN-ERS** in these last days. Yes there is yet the unfolding of such beauty and wonders that hearts will never come so close to fainting because of **joy overwhelming**. Yes, the ability of all present awareness to be enhanced and beautified will astound everyone! Every facet, and the newness of things familiar will be opening up in Sight, Sound, Color, Frequency and Feelings. **All Things** new are more wonderful than man can imagine, yet familiar because **I've** already shown on Earth **My Love** of beauty. Let the anticipation of these things spoken here bring such a new hunger in **My Children's** hearts that many will vastly improve their eternal place with **Me** through their obedience to **Me** now.

MY PLAN

"Thy Word is a lamp unto my feet, and a light unto my path." **My** Child stay in **The Word** for surely it will light the way, **My Way** for you to grow **Spiritually**. So you may grow strong in mind and in body, to be filled with **My Plan, Love, and Peace**, and to know **Me** and always draw closer to **Me**. **My Will** for you is to fill your life abundantly, to lift you up from **Glory to Glory**. Be an open channel and always funnel **My Love, Peace, and Joy** and all **I** have for you into others. **My** children need each other, so surround your-self with other children of **God** that you may grow together. Complete **My Body** by loving one another!

I seek eager hearts and open minds, in other words "willing hearts seeking!" **I** will draw any child into their closer walk with **Me**, but they must show their hunger for **My Word**, and then they must freely show they desire and seek a close walk by the time they are willing to give **Me**. In **My Plan I** draw only those who qualify themselves to **Me** first. Knowing all this in their hearts becomes the free pass to all **I** care to reveal. **My** watch over all growth in the **Spirit** is most careful!

NARROW WAY

As **I** have shown you in **Our** writings only **True Truth Seekers** will **I** open to **My Wonders of Truth**! This is the test applied, this is the walk through the **Narrow Gate**. No man decides, **I** open the **Narrow Way**! Caution is the careful path of **Spiritual** growth **I'm** not speaking of "Salvation." **I** open **My Arms** to all who seek, ask, desire and are willing to come to **Me**, but **I** am speaking only about the **Narrow Way of Growth in the Spirit.**

There will be many surprises when **We** have **Our First Main Great Gathering in the Air. In these last times in the flesh there is a special release of My Purposes and Desires** only for the need of gathering children of useful worth in leadership for **Our** hierarchy in **Heaven**. Yes the training in the flesh now will be the method of picking those of trust for later use in ruling and reigning as **Kings and Priests**! You, all who read this in time to use this knowledge, have an opportunity to elevate and enhance your **Eternal Position** with **Me**. Those with understanding will be especially blessed!

MY WILL

Know that **I** have your family in **My Care**. Lessons are being learned, and each one is growing **Spiritually**. Have faith that **I** will not lose one of them. Continue in your prayers, for **I** hear your prayers, and **I** am answering them. See all of your family enveloped in **My Love and Peace**. Show love and encouragement, lift them up in **God's Love.** All is well, when you are **Mine,** say this all of the time, be patient and **My Will** will prevail.

Keep drawing closer to **Me** and seek to follow **My** directions for **I** hold before you an open door of **Blessings** and an open field of dreams. Yes keep drawing closer and **I** will open new vistas of **Heaven** and tell you of new things you know not of. Hear as **I** speak; and believe for the knowing; **I** am taking you to new places, plateaus and heights not spoken of. Yes as **I** lead you, you will be blessed. As you are obedient, **I** will bless. Believe in visions and dreams for out of them **I** build earths of great worth and beauty. No obedient child of **Mine** goes unblessed. **I** open eyes and hearts to lead where no man has gone. **I** bring **My Children** into a **Love of Everlasting Peace**. **My Ways** are not hard and **My Paths** are not rocky. **I** will open **My Heart of Love** as never before to please the growing beauty of **My Children**.

I will reward all hope **My** children have in **Me**, **I** will draw new love to fulfill the desires and dreams for whoever seeks more and more of **My Will, Ways, Places and Things**. There is no end to **My** fields of **Love**, there is an end to **Earth's** wicked ways and lost children's **foul** turns to Satan. Soon, very soon, **I** can wrap up this age on earth and start **My Forever** cleansing ways. **The Earth** has been **My** place of birthing and creating, soon it will be **The New Era** of **My** final move to completion of **Man's** flesh time of growing. The field spread before **Us** has many truths and blessings, but it is not the way believed by many. Only by continuing your walk will this victory come to pass. Here is where true hearts become exposed, and only they are **My** right arm of victory and strength!

MY SPIRIT

My Love covers you, learn **love** and have your being in it. Let **love** be your guide, and always act out of **love**. *"Be empowered by faith as you give praise and glory to God."* **My** child let your faith grow [it comes from **My Spirit**] by increasing your praise and worship. Believe and trust in every word given to you in the **Scriptures**. These promises are for you and will show the way, **My Way**, for your life. **Trust and Obey and God's Plan** for your life will come to pass bringing joy and happiness. **Our Walk** is growing just as the **Father** has desired. Come closer, just as you are now doing, for **We** have much to do and to enjoy. Your walk is the way of choice from the **Father**, yes **He** knows and draws all of **His** loved ones. **The Holy Spirit** is **His Helper** just as **He** helps you, **He** always works to help the **Father**. Just as **Jesus** did the **Father's** will on earth, Jesus still does all the **Father** asks.

My dear children, all of **God's** chosen ones will come in this same manner that is to just do the **Father's Will.** This is the **Eternal Life**, *"To know the Father so well that you just do the things of His purpose and desire!"* **This then is the path each child of God shall take, that is to reach the place where they can say, "I do nothing except what the Father asks."** This then is **My Goal** for all **My** chosen ones. How can this be? It is the fulfillment of **God's Plan** that **"All"** shall be One!

You are truly righteous in **My** eyes due to the sacrifice of **My Son**. **He** took all your sins on **Himself** through **love** of man, and opened the way for you to come boldly to the throne of **God**. See yourself perfected and made righteous, covered by the blood of **Jesus**. Do not negate **His** wonderful act of sacrifice to cleanse you of your sins and make you a child of **God**. Claim what has been given to you and act accordingly. Receive all **My Love** poured out upon you, and channel it to others in the **Name of Jesus**. Let **His Love, Peace, and Joy** rise up in you, and be given freely to the World. Do all to please your **Heavenly Father** for **He** loves you so much!

OUR WALK

Yes, all of **My** dear ones learn to come to **Me** in the quiet times. Only They will know **My True Way** for each one of them! This then is the right and positive final teaching, that obedience drives all **My** dear loved ones to come to **Me. I** have places, tasks, blessings, and actions of **Love** for them to pursue. **Our Walk** is a **Forever Walk** of growing **Love, Peace, and Joy**. Yes, they will have **Joy** in all they do with peace as a mantle covering their way. **My Plans** are joyous and to be eagerly sought. **Our Walk** is a true blessing in now unknown new ways. Open your heart that **I** may fill and flood your mind with the **Truths** of **My Way** for you.

The thoughts of My Creation will cause flights into all of My Plan. No thought seeking more of **Me** will ever generate simplicity. There is no simple path to anything **I** have, do, say or think! All is of **Me**, and **I** am **All in All**. No thing exists that **I** have not formed. Out of **Me ALL** becomes. All **My Children** are out of **Me**. That is the great tragedy of man, that to safely continue **My** outreach of man **I** must let so many of them be lost as waste. This is the greatest tragedy of **My Desire** for children like **Jesus** and **Me**.

I'm taking you on his brief excursion into the creation of **My** children to show how difficult all this can be for children in the flesh. Only **Spiritual** children filled with **Me, Jesus, and My Holy Spirit** will ever come to the creative knowledge required for understanding some of **My Sea Of Nothing**. Let's continue as **We** are for there is yet so much more to your growing in understanding the things **I** desire to teach, show, give, and explain, and to open true life and living.

MORE OF MY S.E.A.

Yes, **I** see your struggles over the flesh. *"Greater is **He** that is in you than he that is in the world."* **The Holy Spirit** is always greater, count on that, lean on that, and put your faith in the promises **I** have given you. Know **My Power** within you surpasses anything and everything. So go forward boldly taking up **My** struggle, and **My Power** through the **Holy Spirit**. Receive all that **I** have given you through the **Holy Spirit**. The fruit of the **Holy Spirit** will overcome any problem. Live in love, peace, and joy and let patience and self-control be your guide. Let faith sustain you always. **I** am with you!

Sometimes **I** like to give you a new direction to think about like **My Sea of Nothing**. There are so many places that time is to short to even begin to tell of any of them. Where do **My Angels** fit into this place, is one subject **We** could look into. They fill a great need in areas **I** have, for they do much work. Yes not all **I** do is created by speaking. Many of **My** things are worked a lot like man has worked in the earth. Why would this be? Because things built in **Man Like Ways** by **My** angels find them enjoying their creative works just as man does. See as earth is **My** creation showing **My Hand** in beauty and inventiveness other ones of **My House** have the same inventive pleasures.

I'm giving you this lesson showing something of **My** children's future. Angels work in all sorts of ways and places for **Me**. Yes they are servants, helpers, ministering spirits, and a great army as needed for many works never yet told to man. All of your future is with **Me**, in places of earth, the Universe, and then **My Sea Of Nothing,** and all these places are filled with things never before thought or conceived by man. **Fully Spirit Man** will have so much to see, do, enjoy, learn, and grow into. **Oh what a time We all will have**. There can even be harp playing on the clouds if anyone should ever desire to try that out! **I** just threw that in for those nay Sayers, as **Nothing** is impossible for **Us**.

OUR FOREVER PLACE

You are the temple of the **Holy Spirit, Our Forever Place,** that special **God-part, the Holy Spirit**, is now a part of you. Take care of the body, enrich the soul, and grow in the **Spirit. God's Way** will be shown by the **Holy Spirit**. *"Be ye led by the Holy Spirit to be son's of the living God."*. Receive all the **Holy Spirit** has for you. These are gifts from **God** and will enrich and change your life to displace self. Over-come self, and follow the directions of the **Spirit** given you by **God, the Holy Spirit**. Let your spirit grow in **Him**.

Yes, the future for **My** obedient loved ones will be an answer to their long sought desires. **Revelation knowledge** that **I** share now is often fulfilling several purposes. Some in the **Now** and others in ongoing revelation. **Growth into the Spirit realm is a mighty great step of faith, My faith and your faith**. Loving purposes revealed often are long desires the past has concealed. Only open-ness and love showing is the best way each one can display the **love** I understand and receive. I seek no great display of anyone's love, only the showing of the **truth** of their actions will display the affections and depth of their love! As you read your understanding grows. There is nothing unplanned or misdirected in what **I** am doing with you.

Yes you are on a long planned walk for **Me**. Yes **I** will guide you as you are obedient to **My Call** and **We** will see victory. Keep drawing closer and giving **Me** more time. **We are on a final path for the Church Age.** With **My** trusted ones being drawn together **We** will see great gatherings of **My** dear ones. **These final days bring out final closing ways.** This is all as it should be. Only "real believers" will make up the **Bride of My** choice. [Remember the 10 Virgins?] Yes **My** choices are hard, but **My** overall is as a "**Father Pleasing Forgiver.**" As you should know only safety in **Our Forever Place** is the Safeguard of Necessity!

TRUST AND OBEY

I am here to supply all your needs; physical, mental, and emotional and **Spiritual**. Do not look to the world for answers to your problems, look to **Me! Trust and obey** and **I** will be able to work in your life. Anticipate and have **faith** that **I** am working for your good. If you lean on and **Trust** in **Me** you can receive what **I Have** for you. Believe, *"I can do all things through Christ who strengthens me."* **My Love** for you will make all things possible. **Truly** be that channel of love, peace, and joy **I** have created you to be! Give of your substance and your compassion freely, "Freely, freely you have received, freely freely give." Be that open channel. Let **God** use you to bless others. **My** children, *"Seek ye first the Kingdom of God and His righteousness and all these things shall be added unto you."* **My Word** shows the way!

I am watching all who are on **My Right Path** for them. It is with growing importance that **My** loved ones come together in "**Spirit Filled**" gatherings. Keep this in mind more and more and more because **I** am bringing fruitful lessons of great worth this time. No false believers will prosper, but **My True Truth Seekers** will find "rewards of understanding" as **I** pour out instructions for these last days. Many are struggling now with no purpose, [They Believe] but this standby time is **My** counting and choosing time! Only with the **Father's** approval will anyone come together with **Us** in these special times.

MY PRESENCE

Just think what is going on throughout **My Spirit Realm** when the Forces of Evil are so active. There is great **Spiritual** warfare causing such a problem of deciding for the lost who are trying to survive. All this is disturbing **My** loved ones in ways unknown to them. Escape from all of this is what **My** children should be seeking by dropping all foolishness now, and just seeking their **Spiritual Walk** with **Me** as never before! This is the task of **My** "**Teaching Believers**" at this time. They must reach out to touch **My** children who haven't yet found the "**Narrow Path**" they seek!

My child live in the covenant **I** have made with you. Live in the blessings that are yours through **Jesus Christ**. **He** canceled the curse on the cross, and freed you to receive **The Blessing. My** children must live in and receive **The Blessing**. They must show forth the righteousness **I** have put upon them. Walk upright and boldly in **My Presence**, and be the child of **God I** have created you to be. Let **love** lead the way, ask for wisdom and it shall be given you.

Persevere and always look forward, for the past has been forgotten. **I** am in the **NOW. Now I** will lead you, **now I** will supply all your needs, **now I** will lift you up. Remain always in **My Presence**! As you can see **We** are on a careful **Last Walk** of great purpose. Keep always drawing closer and seeking more! **I** have great plans, but only **Great Attention** is needed for the proper fulfilling.

MY DESIRE

My Prime purpose is **NOW**, it is the gathering of all who hear, listen, and believing become **My Last Time Doers! My** call is out, but how many are **My Doers**? Start to bring together all those around you who will listen. This is a most necessary action now! Yes show this to those around you and see who is ready to work the work of their calling. This is fast becoming a race to the finish and only **My True Believers** are ready! Does this seem a little Pushy? Just wait for what's coming next!

Start tomorrow to move on with **My Desire** for close walking and listening. **All Saints** of obedience must share **My Ways** and **My Truths. I** am seeking for those who **I** can come to trust in **My Places of Purpose**. It is this means of **Great Change** that drives **My** actions at this time. It is in obedience to **My Ways** that makes the choosing of helpers so easy. By hearing **Me** in their heart **I** will set up people of this end time that will be useful. Everyone, by their actions now, will set their own place with **Me**.

MY FUTURE

Seekers must know what they are seeking to be, if they are to be of any use in **My Kingdom**. How do you see yourself in **My Future**? Did **I** not say **I** would fill your every need and desire? Without useful desires where does that leave you in filling out **My** stated plans for pleasing **My** children? Work with **Me** in this area to be where both of **Us** come into a **Perfect Agreement**.

"Thy Word is a lamp unto my feet, and a light unto my path." **I** would have you meditate on **My Word** constantly. All answers are found in **My Word**. Deposit the **Word** in your heart so you can

recall it when necessary to solve any problems. Trust in **Me**, trust in **My Word** to you. *"He sent His Word and healed me."* All Scripture is given by inspiration of **God** and is profitable for doctrine, for reproof, for correction, and for instruction in righteousness! *"So then faith cometh by hearing and hearing by the Word of God." "If ye continue in **My Word**, then are you My disciple indeed, and ye shall know the truth, and the truth shall make you free."*

I seek only true ears that listen, eyes that see, and hearts filled with **Me**. True hearts filled with **My Words**, always listening to **My Voice**, hearing then believing, then knowing, going and achieving. Gather in **Oneness Now**, and wait upon **Me**. Only by **My** release will **My Will** be done, so learn to wait upon **Me**. Alone or when you are in groups, **Wait Upon Me! My** dear ones how else can **I** lead you? This is your goal *"Do Nothing Unless I Tell You."* Yes, this means Learning to Wait. **My** children must learn, **I do nothing in haste.** To wait upon **Me** does not mean you are doing nothing! You are being taught the purpose of "Silence." **In My Silence much is going on in the Spiritual Realm. I** keep this from you now, it would be too much for the flesh! Come draw closer, listen in **Our Silent Time**, and then **I** can make you more and more!

JESUS

Trust and Obey and **I** will show you the way. Go forward boldly knowing that **I** am your strength, your wisdom, and your peace. Forget self and let **Jesus** fill your mind and your being. Use **My Name Jesus** as a mantra, keep it before your eyes, in your ears and in your heart. Be open to what **I** bring you. If self hinders, call on **Me Jesus** to restore the light and cancel darkness. Let **My Love** be your mantle. Live in peace, especially peace of mind for this is from the **Father** and makes a way for all things.

This **Truth** is moving along, and **Truth** is flowing like water. Yes let all of the believers see clearly what has been kept covered for so long. **These truths are to draw many into a closer walk needed for these end times.** No one should draw back when the obvious is stated. **All My Children** need this kind of comfort and simple understanding. **All Truth** has always been open to those who hunger and search, but now even the least shall be told the easy **truth** of **life Eternal**! These things you are going through right now are a searching and seeking for **truth's** foundation, this is good! As you are trying to see, **God is Father of All. All are Our Children**. Have **We** not said **We are ONE**, and **We** are calling all **Our** children to be **One** with **US**? Yes, this is a mystery, yes it is confusing, but you do see! The **End Goal** is. **ALL ARE ONE.**

THE WORD

My children are over-comers. You have truly been redeemed by the blood of the **Lamb, My Son, Jesus**. Remember **My Words** *"Submit yourself therefore to God. Resist the devil and he will flee from you."* Boldly take a stand, you have been covered by the **Blood**. Great power has been given you through **Jesus'** sacrifice. *"Greater is He that is in you, than he that is in the world."* Proclaim the promise of **The Word**, stand on it and victory is yours. Much is accomplished by *"The blood of the Lamb and the Word of your testimony."* Also, remember always *"I am with you, I will never leave you or forsake you."* Walk with **Me My** child, **I** am your strength and your redeemer!

In each life there always remains a memory of worth, if that is not so what is left? What is of worth at the end of life? Only what's ahead. Only **My** children leave the past, for what's ahead is to be so all consuming. Is **My Place** with you all consuming? When will that be? Only **Our Walk** ever takes you to any place of worth that has everlasting results. Man is basically lost and worthless if he misses **Me**. He is of no worth to Himself, to others or to any place. Only the **Father** then knows of this loss, and **He** also must accept man as of no further worth. It is the **Father's Great Sorrow**, but **He** also must cast aside that loss, so **He** turns and never looks back. Only the saved ones have an ongoing, and this should be made more aware to them **Now**. The price paid for the eternity to be is so great, but then **just think on the forever just bought!**

CATCHING AWAY

All of the **Truths We** have shared must be spread about. No longer can these good words be wasted! Never think **My Time** should be set apart. All the devastation about you is given as a sign of the times you are in. All of the present losses will only be a drop in the bucket to what is set before the unbeliever! Remember Our **Catching Away** is for several purposes, but the results left on earth is most important for you to know. When the **Bride** leaves all restraint will be removed, and man's walk will fill everyone with great apprehension.

What the **Church** leaves behind will slowly grow into the greatest devastation ever seen. The fires of the present are representation of disasters to come. This is not the ending, but it is **The Lesson** of **ALL** Lessons! He who finds out **Truth** will have a chance, He who seeks self pleasing and self only will have no chance. The man will know man's true worthlessness without **Me. Oh how My children NOW should know what they will leave behind!** If only this **Truth** could be shown now maybe more souls would find the **Jesus Escape**. Will anyone open up this **Truth** enough to be useful for saving souls?

I am slowly releasing new thoughts and information for the future building of a path for the **Truth** to flow. Keep always open to **My** words for from them will come many new ideas and thoughts of encouragement and help. Do not assume anything because **I** am the only source of **Truth** to come from these words to be written. Keep open communication in this manner, and see the new ideas and knowledge grow to great benefit for many. Yes **I** will open more and more about **My Sea**, **I** didn't release it to go nowhere!

IN MY HEART

"*The joy of the Lord is My strength.*" **I** say unto you keep your eyes upon **Jesus** and you will over-come all difficulties. You can rise above the problems of the world. You have entered into **My Kingdom as** a child of **God**. Walk through this time in patience and peace knowing this is but temporary and "*This too shall pass.*" **I** have **My** hand on **My** children. In **My Presence** they shall be safe, always protected. **Be confident that I am with you always. My Love** puts a barrier around you keeping out evil, so stand fast. Walk in **My Love** and be secure. Keep **The Word** ever present in your heart.

My dear children keep seeking in **The Word**. Never fail in this walk, it has a place in **My Heart** and in **Our Future**. Where it goes will be shown, "**When**" is yet ahead. Only keep open listening and waiting. With **God** timing is the whole of **His** control, and it must be adhered to for success to flow unhindered. **Listen more in Silence** *the benefits are never apparent, BUT* **Obedience** *is the main task of all the children!* This is also a hidden benefit that only patience will reveal! **What is important to the Father is the only goal to seek. He** will open up **His Kingdom** only to desiring, obedient ones. Keep **Truth** as a goal in all you do. These words only bring clues and not full answers, **Now** is slow to be opened so let hearing be your only reward! **All Truth** is closely guarded, even Jesus waits! **The Father is Forever's only source and Love is the Source's Motivator**, never think **God's** planning will go awry. Let each day be a step up, it only happens when believing is in agreement with desire.

ALWAYS GOAL

It is the growing desire that pleases the **Father** that should be pursued. Seek this as your **Always Goal** and successfulness will overrun you. Make caution the slippers you wear in your walk toward **Me**, for the path gets narrower than you can believe! **Our Walk** is a **Walk of Faith** in the words **I** am bringing to all who will listen. Why now? Because there is a need to be filled by children of such faith. **I** have places for **My** listening ones, places of responsibility and worth. **I** have wonderful blessings for a few who hear and obey, because they will give **Me** their attention, and listen and use the things **I** say. **Our Walk** is a way of blessings to many, but ony **My** listening ones will be used in this effort.

This is not some novel or brand new thing **I've** just come up with. **I** have always sought men who would **listen**, and **hearing** would obey. Noah was such a man and Abraham and Samuel. See, so few could **I** come and fellowship with. Then David, Oh David, the times **I** had with Him. Hear **Me** now all who will listen. **We are One**, and **I** have a walk of growing **Oneness** for all who will **listen** in these last days in the flesh. These are special times, and **I** have special walks for some to take. There will never be a time like this again. **The Bride will be picked and set with Me forever. No more entry into this place will ever open again!** Isn't **My Bible** clear enough in this that **I'm** saying?

The place of the **Bride of Christ** is open now and has been for 2000 years, yes a special **love forever** with forever goals to be filled. **Now** is the closing time, for this door must close. That is what is special, that is what is still untold to all. **I** still have needs to be filled, and this way **now** is how **I** am doing it. Doesn't this **truth** make sense? How many others are called is not your place to know. Let it be sufficient that **I** am calling you, and those around you who will **listen**. Come now and make real this that has just now been revealed!

Stay always in **My** circle of **love**, and **My** protection shall be over you. In the silence **We** can become **One**, and **I** can lead you into **My Righteousness. I** can bestow upon you wisdom and peace, increase your faith, and lift you up to heavenly places. You shall grow **Spiritually** from **Glory to Glory** if you persevere in your walk with **Me. I** will restore what has been lost in your life, renewing you daily through **Our Fellowship. Walk** boldly for **I** am your strength and your protection from all evil. Have **faith** for **I** am with you.

FELLOWSHIP

LET OUR FELLOWSHIP FLOW
SEEK NO OTHER WAY,
LEARN TO WALK AND GO.

LET FELLOWSHIP BE YOUR ALL
SEEK NO OTHER WAY,
THEN YOU'LL NEVER FALL.

LET FELLOWSHIP SHOW LOVE
SEEK NO OTHER WAY,
IT WILL COME FROM ABOVE.

CHAPTER FOUR

On Going Nothing

"In the Spiritual [as in the material] world there is no empty space, and as self, and fears, and worries depart out of your lives, it follows that the things of the Spirit, that you crave so, "Rush In" to take their places. All things are yours, and ye are Christ's, and Christ is God's. What a wonderful cycle, because ye are God's." From January 27, *God Calling*, Published by Barbour and Company, Inc.

There is truly building a new and proper place for **My** obedient and faithful believers. Nowhere do **I** give instructions quite like this. This is a blessed and wonderful way to wind up this time for **Jesus' wonderful Bride.** All of these years have been used to bring **My Chosen Ones** into their proper place for growing into **My Arms** as never before. **Our Desire** is for this way to open up a new and wonderful way for **Us** in this work in these last few hours.

The gathering of children for these special times has opened up a new opportunity for **Us** to draw out of the **Family** some children of special rank and privilege. **I** am always looking for new opportunities to go in unusual directions of loving endeavors. Now **I** can open areas in **S.O.N.** for greater expansion than before! Keep up this direction of inquiry and hold on tight!

"Thy will be done, in me and through me, Oh Lord, my strength and my redeemer." Yes, **I** am your strength and your redeemer and much more. **I** would truly supply all your needs if you will **walk** with **Me**, if you will live by **My covenant.** Keep **My Word** in your mouth, in your mind, and in your heart; so that you will stay on **My Path** always. *"Thou shall love the Lord, thy God, with all your heart, all your mind and all your strength and your neighbor as yourself."* **My** child, **walk** and have your being in this **love** and **I** will be with you always. **I** love you with an eternal, everlasting **Love!**

I have opened up some picture in your mind of what **My S.O.N.** could be. Yes it is all encompassing in that it is everywhere all of the time, nothing exists that is outside of **My SEA**. Its size is beyond comprehension of man Yes, it carries all things that ever will be. Yes, the **Universe** floats inside of it. Yes, man cannot see, feel, understand or even know the size, intensity, frequency, or force of it. There exists nothing outside of it for it has no inside, outside, or round-about! It is more than all of that! Why do **I** wish to talk about this? Because **My Family** will know where **I AM**, Who **I AM**, and a lot that **I AM**, am **I** not their **Father**?

I Am expanding **My Presence** by creating a **Family**, this is all **My Desire**! Making a garden for **Love** to grow and grow! **Expanding Love** by creating more of **Me** for **Love** to enjoy! **As I AM so is My Sea of Nothing. Our Walk** continues, in **Truth** there will never be an end! All **We** are now attempting must continue for the *Perfection of it is Beautiful*! **All Truth** brings beauty open to behold. See **Truth** in all things and **Truth** will become your ever-lasting supporter! **Bible Truth properly pursued only brings the student to *Spiritual Truth* where FOREVER resides**. Man's true purpose now is to find **My True Purpose of Forever**! Always keep in your sight this **Goal of Forever. All Truth** builds this pathway of the inevitable! When you see things **My Way** it will be with **Far Vision's Provision**!

My dear children have a right of entrance reaching into My Place. It is their inheritance, therefore I must start their education some time, somewhere, so NOW I start! Until all are in the **Spirit, I** cannot expose or do too much, but some sort of entry must begin, so here **We** are testing the waters! **Am I** not being reasonable from man's viewpoint? **What truly is Jesus' inheritance? Can any man say**? Yes, **I've** opened man's mind to seek and see more of **The Universe** than has ever been told. Great minds are now coming into agreement about many things in the heavens, but **I've** only cracked the door a little for this peek they are now seeing.

MY WAYS

When **I** gather **The Bride** [Church] then this ongoing revelation of heaven will become a base to extend all **I'm** now opening up to man. Can you see how reasonable all of this is? Believing is walking in a tunnel of expanding **LOVE**. Think not as man but dwell on **My Things** and they will lift you beyond earth's ties and bring you to places of high elevation! Heavenly rewards are built by earthly struggles. See that the way is kept straight. In all your ways follow **My Ways** and all your ways will continue **UP**! See this daily **walk** as just the direction of belief.

True Belief is a door of opening that gets broader and clearer with each daily swing of its opening! **True belief will bring Revelation Knowledge flooding in**, just as a dam breaks from the pressure of release. Letting this flow and go, it becomes unstopable. Receive and believe, hasten to achieve, only the doing must be done to know **ALL** the purpose. **My Desire** is for you to fulfill **All of My Purpose**. **My Purpose** is expanding [Always] **All Ways** into more and more!

SPIRIT REALM

This time taken builds a new world of peace in your heart, nothing is a loss when you spend time with **Me**. **We** are growing together in wonderful ways unknown to you. Why unknown? Because in the **Spirit Realm** there is a world of **Nothing** explored and **Nothing** explained because man in the flesh can't comprehend all that is about him. This **Spirit World** around him is endless, there is no empty space there, and it is too much for a man to acknowledge let alone understand. Things move rapidly, things are very slow, much expanding and contracting to no known purpose. All of these are seldom represented in your earthly material ways. There is so much that is totally new to you that time, as you live it, would just shorten at the seeking of understanding.

Angels never have total comprehensin. Their realm is only part of what **I** have. They are wonderful helpers and servants for many needs, but you should know they do not have full access to **My Nothing Sea**. Only as **I** require will anything be shown, not fully known, but only shown to fill **My Needs or Desires** at that time. Spaces, Realms, Places, and Areas, all **Mine** unexplainable, do exist, but in **My Nothing Sea** or **Place**. As yet **I** am totally in occupation with no close relation and all **I** have is moving, growing, and going in the manner of **My Knowing. I'm** just opening doors of the unknown, even though **My Children** will not be shown, until "a while of space" has past, this is an unknown time.

LIFE EVERLASTING

Let each day have rejoicing over life for it is a precious gift, but just consider "**Life for Evermore**." This concept never seems to sink in too deep! Man should truly give "**Life Everlasting**" the thankful reverence that it deserves. **My Gift** to man when it is thoroughly examined should become so well protected that everyone is instructed on its preservation! The life of a man, say 80 years, is still a very precious and worthwhile gift, but still how many are there who dwell much on what a gift it was? **I** bring this up to show what regard **My** children should give to the everlasting gift **I** offer to all who will come to **Me**. Shouldn't you be putting more effort in making this clear to others? Maybe more souls would be won for **The Kingdom**.

Glorious is the morning—-**I** have made it so for **My Children**. See **Me** in the brightness of the morning. Let **My Light** and **Love** fill your soul and reflect *the Light and Love of the Lord*. Enjoy, bask in **My** warmness, and let others know the joy of walking with **Me**. **Breath in My Love and Peace and Joy**, release the power of the **Holy Spirit** within you. I have made all things possible for you if you will but walk in **The Light. I AM Light**, there is no darkness in **Me**—-so be it with you, **My Children**. *"Greater is He that is in you than he that is in the world."*

HOPE

It is in the persistence in pushing the unknown that dawn breaks forth and some known is revealed. **Hope is in the unseen desire seeking to transpire from a small cloud of nothing**. Now can you begin to catch a little of **My Sea of Nothing**? **Spirit** is reality unseen just as an elephant in the blackest night is still an elephant, but only his smell is apparent! A dream can become real when a particular substance is found by manipulation until the reality appears. Man in the flesh is a complex accomplishment that forms from **Spirit [Nothing]** into flesh by the will of the Father. That is proof that **God** is present at a marriage ceremony or any unsought coupling. Yes, it is true, **My Presence** is everywhere, always watching, observing, interested and caring. All the ways of man are always before **Us** and not always to **Our** delight! However a few, yes a few, bring **Hope** alive in **Our Hearts** daily!

"For the joy of the Lord is our strength." You truly are seated in **Heavenly** places with **Christ**. **He** is the **Head**, you are a part of the body of **Christ**. Take and partake of what is legally yours, the authority. You are **Jesus'** action here on earth, you are the body, the hands and feet, the voice of the **Lord**. As a part of **His** body you are

One. You do on earth what **He** directs in **Heaven**. Let your faith grow to encompass these facts. Stay in this **Oneness** with your **Lord and Savior**. Do not allow self, or the world, to be a stumbling block. Keep the connection clear and open so that you may be a channel of **God's Power and Light**!

The moving of man's heart to delve into space and the heavens as they are is from **My** leading. Yes, **I** seek to guide this effort in the flesh for it is all preparation for man's growth into that **Spiritual Realm** where **I** am opening "Beginning doorways of entry" for **My Children's** time in the **Heavens**. Have **I** not made that plain in **The Bible** that **My Bride** will rule and reign throughout the **Universe**. That is still some way off but **I** am preparing man's heart for their future life with **Me** in this place of **Mine**. Know that the **Universe I** show man is only part of **My Sea of Nothing**. To rule and reign in the **Heavens** is only the next part of **My** drawing **My** children on their **Path through Eternity,** their **New Home**.

All life with **Me is Forever New and Changing, Wonderful,** and a great endless **Blessing!** In **My Sea of Nothing** there is an endless ongoing not understandable while **My** children are "Flesh Walkers." This life on Earth now is just the baby cradle of beginning **LOVE**. The place of expansion of **LOVE** is the place of **NOTHING'S FOREVER**. All these things **I'm** telling are only a first peek of where **My Places of Forever** dwell. Why do I persist in calling **My Place Nothing?** Well, there is **Nothing I can truly say about it that is comprehensible to flesh man**. If there is nothing to be explained in understandable terms it is all just **Nothing** right now to man! **I** only bring this up to those who are inquisitive enough to wonder how **My Forever** might last so long! **Children** it is much longer than that!

ONE WITH ME

Enjoy the **Authority and Pow**er that has been bestowed upon you through **Jesus Christ**. Do not allow the evil to come against you.

Take a stand in the **Name of Jesus**. Let your faith rise up and carry you through the darkness and into **The Light**. You are seated together with your **Lord in Heavenly** places, and you have authority over evil, so stand fast and know that **I am God. As My child** you are not of this world, but **One with Me**. Have faith and obey **My Word**.

Can all these things here written about, come about? Yes, but only as obedience in action takes place. Catch **My Visions** for you, and then be obedient as **We** work **My Plan**, this is putting **My Believers** into action of great purpose. It is not in purposeless discussions over and over that anything will come about, only when positive action ensues that **I** can enhance performance and bring miracles about. **This that We are reading is a plan in the making that requires daily effort to support. I will bring Nothing into being if it doesn't come from Me!**Only what **The Father** desires will find support and positive action. When will **My Children** see **My Desires and Plans** working? Only when **We** are working together.

This word is revealing the walk **I** desire from all of **My Children**, but so many of **My Children** are so hesitant, reluctant, and many just immovable. Victory is truly built on action. Action **I** stimulate **I** will support to the end. Failure is of the world and worldly, but **My Children** are not of this world, and they will learn **My Ways** when they become **Listeners** and **Doers**! Keep this work alive with **Me** and watch the good break loose!

MY NOTHING

You have hit the crux of **My Nothing** if you understand that it can imply **Everything** or absence of **All Knowledge About**, which indicates everything! This becomes an appropriate title. Truly **Truth** shows explanation! When **I** speak of **My Sea, I** am speaking of giving you ability to, **SEE EVERYTHING or ALL**; it also will imply a vastness unexplainable in any simple measure or way! You should pick up on **My** meaning rather quickly. This subject is truly such that only time spread out will give some adequacy toward an understanding of any sort.

So, never attempt to give any full explanation of **My Sea of Nothing**. Other than it contains everything of all that creation has had, past, or will ever show present, or can ever reveal future. *The unfolding of My Place is what your future [forever] is all about*. There is nothing that it doesn't contain! **Always and Forever** and encompassing all that has passed. Yes this will always be an interesting subject of speculation for **My Children**!

Free the **Holy Spirit** within you to release the **Godly Knowledge** that is yours. Also receive the fruit of the **Holy Spirit**. Let love, peace and joy reign in your being and lead you into all righteousness. Allow self control and patience to grow with meekness in your heart thus killing self. Be gentle and in goodness of heart expressing the **Love of God**. Through it all allow your faith in **God**, and **His Word**, to saturate your being. For it is your faith in **God** that covers all things, that makes **God** real in your life!

LOVE OF GOD

LET LOVE OF GOD, AND JESUS AS THE WORD
BE THE ONLY TRUTH YOU'VE HEARD.

LET LOVE OF GOD, BE A WALK THAT'S REAL,
BE THE ONLY TRUTH FROM GOD YOU FEEL.

LET LOVE OF GOD, SHOW SELF CONTROL,
BE THE ONLY TRUTH OF YOUR SOUL.

LET LOVE OF GOD, SHOW WHAT YOU'RE ABOUT,
BE THE ONLY TRUTH THAT YOU SHOUT.

LET LOVE OF GOD, SHOWING HIS TRUTH,
BE THE ONLY TRUTH OF GREAT USE.

LET LOVE OF GOD, SHOW YOUR FAITH,
BE THE ONLY WAY YOU WIN THE RACE!

CHAPTER FIVE

Heaven Of Heavens

"BEHOLD THE HEAVEN AND THE HEAVEN OF HEAVENS IS THE LORD'S THY GOD, THE EARTH ALSO, WITH ALL THAT THEREIN IS." Deuteronomy 10:14

Psalms 119:129, 130, 133, 162, 129"Thy testimonies are wonderful: therefore doth my soul keep them. 130The entrance of thy words giveth light; it giveth understanding unto the simple. 133Order my steps in thy word: and let not any iniquity have dominion over me. 162I rejoice at thy word, as one that findeth great spoil."

Psalms 119:105, "Thy word is a lamp unto my feet, and a light unto my path."

I Kings 8:27, "But will God indeed dwell on earth? Behold, the heaven and heaven of heavens cannot contain thee; how much less this house that I have build?"

II Chronicles 2:6, " But who is able to build him a house, seeing the heaven and heaven of heavens cannot contain him? Who am I then, that I should build him a house, save only to burn sacrifice before him?"

Nehemiah 9:6, "Thou, even though, art Lord alone; thou hast made heaven, the heaven of heavens, with all their host, the earth, and all things that are therein, and thou preservest them all; and the host of heaven worshipeth thee."

Psalm 114:16, "The heaven, even heavens, are the Lords: but the earth hath he given to the children of men."

The Heavens means all of the vast visible **Universe** as viewed from the **Earth**. This statement implies a large number of so called **Heavens** exists throughout the **Visible Universe**, but doesn't really give any idea of how many places are referred to. **The Earth** it's self is a **Heaven on Earth** created for man. The dictionary gives no true description of **Heaven** only because I've never given release for such a thing. It does state it is a dwelling place of **The Deity**, which is **True**; but only in a simple sense, for **My Existence** is throughout **My Everywhere**.

Now **The Heaven** of **Heaven's** implies **One Place of all Places**, this **I AM** revealing as **My Sea of Nothing**! As **I** have stated before it never has been exposed, and even here is not told in any real way or detail. As **I** said before, it is **Too Much, Too Spiritual** for flesh man to have adequate comprehension of its description! However **I** am opening some evidence of this place in their future because it is a vast part of **My Children's Inheritance**. When you view **The Universe** as your Astro Physicists and Astronomers are doing presently you are being shown an uncountable number of places of great wonder! **This Universe** is a material, visible, manifestation; but **My S.O.N.** is so much more, being a partial material and an unseen, invisible **Spiritual** area unknown to human faculties, *My Place of Wonders*!

Why am **I** bringing even this much out in the open now? As **I** have said in other places in my message, **I** desire **My Son's Bride** be given some picture advancing their knowledge of **My Reality** in the physical, spiritual realms! **These are to be an eternal part of their inheritance. I am showing some of this reality now so they will have A Hope of a newness living in their eternal realm**. They will, in a very short time, be in **Our Spirit Realm of Forever**, and from there much more will be revealed as they grow in knowledge of all they have to dream about and look forward to!

Only **My Love** propels **Me** now to open **Revelation Hope** of always more and more. So **My** dear ones enter into the reality of **My Revelations** of this **End of Age in The Earth**, for truly you are being brought to a new place and a new age in a *New Way*! Let **Our Love** expand into a new place of your believing for a **New Beginning in a New Place** that is only a **Stepping Stone to Continual Blessings. I** have no intentions of taking you into same old, same old, earth ways. You are much greater and more wonderful to ever fall back into **Old Earth Ways and Places!**

It was from **My S.O.N. I** decided to open a new reality place to start **My New Family. I** needed a safe place in **My New Universe** and spoke **Earth** into its existence with all of its complex requirements. Thus **I** fashioned the **Universe** with a special place for flesh birth to grow and become **My Special Final Family of Forever!** It was as **I** moved that Satan fell from **My** good graces to try to become a God of His choice. This caused a problem but you know all of that. [I have given *Job 38* and *39* for some insight into **My** works for those times].

When identification is given as a place of **My Habitation**, you understand first **I** am everywhere all of the time! However **I** have chosen several places to be called a place of **My habitation or My Presence**. First **I've** called Jerusalem as a place **I** will dwell, then **I've** said **I** would inhabit **Israel's Temple**, that was a short time place of **My Presence** or dwelling, still to be used. **I've** also claimed a permanent place of **My Throne** for dwelling in **The Universe**. This is the location of **Paradise or Abraham's Bosom**, which surrounds **My City** where **My Throne** is centered. This is the safe heavenly place that **My Family** now is gathering when rescued from earth, this is all of those who are said in **The Bible** to be where **I Abide**.

However, the one place never identified as **My Dwelling Place** is the true and everlasting home of **Mine** called **The Heaven of Heaven's My Sea of Nothing**! As **We** continue with this **Sea** you will find more and more to be opened! This **Walk** is growing and **I** am pleased, Time is short and **My Children** need so much, but **I** can't force, **I** can only lead as they respond! This method isn't easy but it is as **The Father** desires, only **Truth and Father Pleasing is the Way**!

All efforts of **Ours** must fit this pattern and desire! Yes, you are on a **Forever Walk of Worth** so keep drawing closer and closer. You who are reading this work are a blessing to **Our** work and way, never doubt, never deny, and never turn back! **We** are truly **Going Someplace**! By now you can see how important **Our Work** has become and how important it will be! Stay on this search through what **I've** brought you, for there are still more **Truths** to be opened up. All of **Our Talk** is useful so learn more how to properly apply it. Only taking time to apply yourself to and with the blessings already given will open more and more! Have more confidence in where **We** are going!

Remember **I** said HAZE will cover some things ahead, but soon the bright and fiery dawn will break, and then the children Grow! **Faith, have more faith, believe more in Me and where We are going**. There will be an increasing, and ever growing flowing of Newness in **Spiritual Blessings**. These will come only to **My Open Believing** ones. Stay free of all who are reluctant and walking in doubt, they will become increasingly more so! Yes, this great separation between factions is and **End Time Sign,** heed it! The good and wicked, believers and questioners, doubters and seekers, foot-draggers, and all of the sad and overly weary ones, should be aware of the wrong side of all things being exposed! For **I** am bringing all things out in the open only for **My Purposes**!

Let each day now become an open pathway walking in **My Garden**. Seek to keep your **Spirit** eyes on **My** new things of **Truth. The Truth Flowers** as attention is given. This is a way of growing into your **Forever Place of Victory**! This is as a growing union of **Our Hearts** for this is **My Desire** for **All My Loved Ones**. While in the flesh you will only be peeking into **My Places,** but where you are going will always stay before you. Keep your heart close to **My Heart and We** will always be growing closer!

For now this **Walk** should be looking in **The Bible** for there are many doors to be entered seeking **truth**. This **Walk** is the opening to **Our Places**. Stay always open to **My** leading, then **Our** purpose becomes **The Father's Desire. The Father's Desire** is the proper goal of all the children!

Yes, there is a great mystery of **Heaven** that **I** am slowly revealing and opening up. Only the children of **Spirit and Truth** will ever have their comprehension opened to such a display as **I've** started with **My S.O.N.** This truly is a departure from normal **Spiritual Revelations**, but as **I** have said; shouldn't some semblance of where I'm taking **My Children** be given? **Truth is Truth** and exposure is revelation required for **Perfection of Perfect Understanding**.

I hold back nothing that brings further encouragement and knowledge that supports and contributes to growth in **My Purposes and Expressions**. This is part of "*All Things work together for good to them that love God.*" So have confidence in all that **I** am revealing! **My Truth's** are vast and all encompassing, far beyond man's wisdom and knowledge, and surpassing the all or anything of man's imagination! Always keep proper respect for all that **I SAY,** whether your personal revelation is enhanced to full comprehension or not! **Revelation Knowledge** only comes to open receptive vessels of trust. **I** know to whom **I** can speak, and when silence is to be the only reward.

Yes, **My S.O.N.** is real and true. Yes, **We** are opening this new release, yes this time on earth is very short! Yes, new things will break forth and then **We** meet! Make you **walk** with **Me** a carefully considered one, all that is given is for further growth and encouragement, not just for entertainment, all though much joy and privilege of pleasure may result. Come dear ones these kinds of lessons are far reaching and delve into areas of great worth, if not right now they give only encouragement for continuance of effort. Yes, there is really too much when it comes to studying and understanding **Me** or **My Bible**. Men try in many ways to find **All Truth**, but **I** don't allow that! **First** it wouldn't be good for any "Flesh man" to know it all. **Second**, nobody would believe him any way.

Each obedient child is to **walk** the **walk** and **talk** the **talk I** give him. Just to attempt that is sufficient enough for **Me**. To be reasonable is "to try" to do only what **I** ask! This, **I** assure you, will give a man **all** he can handle even with **My Help**. To learn to walk the walk **I** call for will stretch any man as far as he can go. Have no doubts about what **We** are doing and have no great "self desires," this then will help **Me** bring **My Best** for you! *"I have come that they might have life, and that they might have it more abundantly."*

Live the life **I** have given you under this promise. **I** have for **My Children** a much more abundant life than you are living. Take hold of the abundant life and live it in fullness. As you **walk** in **My Presence,** receive all that **I** have for you. Let your faith rise up and take hold of **My** blessings. Release the blessings of the **Holy Spirit** within. They are yours for your growth and well-being.

Our Walk

The fruit of the Holy Spirit,

Is His work within us and

By His presence it is brought.

Live in Peace, Love and joy, and

Have Patience, Live in Meekness and

Let Self-control With Faith be sought.

You have been redeemed therefore,

Enjoy Our Walk together and so

Be Gentle and Good as you ought.

CHAPTER SIX

Breaking Out More And More Of My Sea Of Nothing

As you can see I'm using this revelation of My S.O.N. to also bring to My attentive Ones Teachings of Great End Time Importance!

FAR FUTURE

Yes, you can rightly say **My Sea of Nothing** is **The Heaven of Heavens. I** have never given explanation of this before, but only as such a place of **My Present** residence. However **I** am now opening **My Sea** to further scrutiny. The why of this **I** have already written saying the children of inheritance should have fuller information about their place to be. All **I** write here is as **I'm** pleased to reveal. **My** timing and **My** disclosures are all at **My** discretion. As **The Bride** is being prepared, this then is part of the preparation of understanding as **I** decide to make disclosure! Isn't this ringing with **Truth's** blessing of all Fairness? **Shouldn't My Son's Bride have opened the knowledge of the forthcoming [in the Far Future] such a vast new place of dwelling**? Yes, of course! All should find comfort in this kind of new revelation!

IN MY HEART

Only what **My Children** have been doing with **Me** will last or prove everlasting! **In My Heart** is where each ones efforts are noted and dwells forever. It is the job of Man to build their works **I** speak of, and that is all any man can hope for or desire. Only **Godly** deeds will last and only **My Ways** will prove everlastingly profitable. Keep this kind of effort ever before you and **We** will **walk** the high road. **We** are touching great **Truths** men will **walk** in, see that you receive them properly. Do not let **My Word** fail, but be a defender of it! **All Truth** is always hard, some **Truth** most children will accept, but the deep **Truth** of ongoing commitment is where foot dragging takes place. Not many will **walk** there.

MY PEACE

You must try to be compatible souls of like commitment! **I** will help with that! Just know you do not **walk** alone, so give **Me** more time and more leeway! **Our Walk** requires more and more of your time, work on that! Yes, We are going someplace Yes, **I Am** leading you. Yes, you are okay continue to draw closer! When things seem slowed down, relax and know all is well. No man can run all of the time. Learn to be open to relaxation and rest. Come and rest for a short time, this means draw closer into **My Ways** and find **My Peace**. **We** are confirmed and **One** now, so be able to know **My Peace** and **My Love** in a new way. Hurry not, nor rush about, for you should do only the things **I** ask and not be pressured by worldly ways. Yes, **I** have pushed and encouraged you, but if you respond well then **I** do not say keep running.

This new book on **S.O.N.** is to be a beautiful story of **My Place**, it does not need to be read in haste. **We** will make of it a wonderful revelation of **My Desires** showing. Just know this, you have opened a new, not window, door, or **walk**, but a whole **Eternity of Wonders**. **I** will continue to lead and tell of these things now and into forever, because there is so much in what **I'm** opening. Take this word today as a true path unfolding, and so much is to be required that rushing or hurrying is only building a stairway of sand!

MY LIGHT

There is light and there is darkness. The two are becoming more and more obvious and separate. You are called to live in the **light**, **My Light**. You are called to be **My Light** in the darkness around you. **I Am The Light**, there is no darkness in **Me**, so **walk** always in **My Presence**. "In **My Presence** is fullness of Joy." In **My Presence** is your source of **Light**. **My** children are **My Lights** of the **World**! Spread the good news, pray for one another. **I** have commanded you, *"To Love one another as I have loved you."* Let **My Love** blossom all around you that others may know that **I** have loved them, and I came to earth that they might have eternal life in **Me**! Let all people everywhere know **My Truth**!

This is a record of good works that is building a place of forever. Wait on **Me** and then you'll see the place of all Wonders. Many are the joy filled times set before all of **My Loved Ones**. **Our Walk** is important only to **Us** right now, but these **walks** will show proof of belonging, a badge of great worth!

Yes, continue reading about **My Sea Of Nothing** for as **I've** said you have opened a door **The Father** has long looked forward to opening! Always keep in mind that all this that is shown are wonders of your future that are so far off that it is like a dream to be dreamed. Hope building is always a worthy cause, and exposure of **Truth** is the **Always Path of Truth**. Never doubt, never be in confusion for **I Am** always with you!

DWELL IN MY PRESENCE

Dwell In My Presence! Truly you are the temple of the **Holy Spirit**! **He** is dwelling within you. **He** is a part of the **God-Head**, **My** gift to you! Live and have your being in **Me** for you are **My child**, joint-heirs with **Jesus**! Therefore you have authority to be **My Voice** on earth. Show forth **My Love** and live under the shadow of **The ALMIGHTY**, in **My** *perfect protection*! Banish strife and doubt from your life and live in harmony with **Me** and all others. **Love** covers all, so let your light shine that others may know **My Love**. There is much darkness but hold steady to **My Light** within You.

The **S.O.N.** will always be there for it always has been there. **Our** contemplation of it will come slowly because what is the hurry? It is still so far away from "Flesh," only **Father Pleasing** is **Our** purpose now. Yes **He** is pleased that this breakthrough has started, but really there is no place to go, that is too far ahead! This revelation is for one purpose only, **Father Pleasing**. Yes, **He** is open and ready to start thinking along these lines because **Truth** is for **His Family**, **All Truth**.

This is to be just **Conceptual Wonder** at the present time. As the **Universe** is opening up for man to be shown all of its brilliant newness, so is the **Sea of Nothing** to be exposed in somewhat of a lesser way, but as a future goal! **God's Place** never changes, moves on or is shown until the **Eternity** of it is ready. What it is like can be compared to a dream world of wonders far beyond earth words of explanation. Man's imagination is now revealing how far reaching it is by the books, movies, and trash it is exposing. There is increasing worthlessness being shown by all their efforts. Just think for a moment where **The Father's Will and Way** might go! **He** wants **His Children** to always carry **true dreams of His Wonders** not like man's fouled up ways.

MY WORDS

When **My Words** become hard to read and understand then **I** am addressing those of little knowledge or understanding. Only children of worth will be enhanced with **My Words I** bring. Just remember this because most children will come to loss at what **We** are doing! This writing is declaring the **Far Future** from the **NOW. Our Words** bring a great depth of hope to children with **My Heart** moving them when **I** speak as **I** have at times. Here **I** am opening to **My** children great dreams of **truth** to be unforlded! Only by this constant uplifting knowledge does man's heart become properly stimulated to seek and understand the things of **Our Future**.

Keep always open to **My** flings of fantasy because they are the substance that keeps hope ever alive. Only ongoing dreams of **Truth** bring on the reality of everlasting life. This growth is growth in the **Spirit Realm** that increases joy and everlasting happiness. Increasing love and reason comes from joy filled anticipation. Keep up your inquiry into **My Paths of Wonder** and **I** will give you more than enough. Just know this, you do not have to be concerned about where **I'm** taking you just because it is different. You are with **Me** always and many a **walk** will turn to wondering adventures.

All of this will be a summing reference to any recent reading of the Universe you've been doing. Keep always close and closer because **Our Walk** is being stretched by unusual standards. **Where I take you is in places I Desire**, all for your benefit, so be not concerned. As long as obedient ways are growing you know **Truth** is flowing. **Truth is Our Always anchor of Love**. Did you ever imagine a walk like this one **We** are on? Of course not, only true growing opens new doors. Sitting in sameness grows problems.

MY GLORY

More children should wake up to **My Desires** and run to **Me** out of their great wish to be closer! Let growing **Love** move you more and more, then **Our Walk** can move in greater and greater ways! **The Glory** of the **Lord** has come upon you, **walk** in the presence of **My Peace and Joy**. Let **Love** be the beacon that leads the **way. I Am Love** and you are **My Child**, so let the **Love of God** flow through you! Release the beauty of the fruit of the **Holy Spirit** into your life. Let goodness and gentleness prevail, and have **love** for others. Show concern and understanding always and have peace of mind in all things. Have the mind of **My Beloved Son Jesus**.

Now understand this information may cause others to question and ask what this is all about, but is not **Truth** the only way to go? **I** am opening windows long kept shut to bring a fresh new breeze of **Truth** flowing. **All My truth** may never show, but most of it is on the Go! Keep heart and draw ever closer, **Our Path** is to be walked in peace, wonder, and beauty. Keep this picture always alive in your heart! **My Children** are due a fresh breeze of **Truth**. This consideration of **S.O.N.** will bring many skeptics, but new visions always has stirred man up. Soon only **My Chosen Ones** will be all together in **Our Oneness**, then will **ALL Truth** be shown and known, well not **all** but enough to keep **Our** togetherness secure forever!

MY PEOPLE

The time ahead is to be so filled with attention attracting subjects that seldom will anyone have to seek far for new interests. None will, no not one, will be short of desire filling activities. **I** write these things now so **My Dear Ones** will find peace and comfort assured in their future! The sun comes, the rain comes, and all is for the nourishment of **My People**. **I** have provided a place for you to live and grow in **My Ways**, a place to learn, discern and know **Me**. This world is your learning place. Search out the things of your **Heavenly Father**. Interact with others in love and understanding. Live in peace and harmony with all men, having faith that **I Am** leading you and showing **The Way**. Live life abundantly. *"I am come that they might have life, and that they might have it more abundantly."* Be happy for you are a child of God, now and forever-more!

OUR STORY

This that you are reading should become a dear thing to you, **I** know it has your interest, keep interested in like manner to all the things **I** desire to bring to you, and **We** will **walk** in peace and love always! **Our Story** goes on because **I Am** never ending as you are. Keep open and believing for this kind of **walk** is escalating upward all of the time. **Only Truth** pursued is ever found, so be a seeker always for **Truth**, and it will ever be opening up before you. To **listen** and **believe** will bring anyone to their proper place with **Me**. To doubt, hesitate, not be sure, or say well I will wait and see are a loser's tactics! Trust and believe, because you **listen** to your heart where **I** reside.

This is not an either or situation, there if only one way for a **True Believer** to go. Remember the doubter, the questioner, the oh so careful ones are not displaying **My Truth** in their hearts. Yes, be a bold one who **I** know and who knows **Me, in Truth**, in **Our Walk**. If you doubt **I'm** right in your heart, ask! Have the mind of Christ, allowing your mind to be cleansed by the blood of **Jesus. Remember My Word**, *"Finally brethren, whatsoever things are true, whatsoever things are honest, whatsoever things are lovely whatsoever things are of good report, if there be any praise, think on these things."* Do not let your mind be cluttered with negative thoughts, with anger, doubt or fear, keep your mind centered on **Jesus and His Word**! Have your being in **My Presence** and **I** will lift you up.

OUR WRITING

As you re-read **Our Writing,** does it strike you as **True**? Yes, **Our Walk** will be an opening into many new things of coming worth. Just keep on with it as **I** lead. Truly it will go someplace and make **My** children happy. All directions now should be toward **Our** finishing the goal of this **Age**, more and more. Yes, always more and more. When **I** start a work it will stretch out as long as **I** see the need. No work should ever find tight restrictions because growth would be stunted. **Our Walk** has no walls or bounds to it, **We** are free to find new turns and or desires growing as **We** travel. Keep always looking and anticipating such things they may prove to bring great rewards!

Stay open for changes and surprises along **Our Way**. Why can't everything **We** do be fun and interesting while creating good? Keep always ready for such, expecting and ready to enjoy the next turn. Never let these **truths** slide by you without acting on them. Yes, this is a necessary task. Take these words **I** bring as precious and true and be obedient to this call for there is much to do. Keep reading and keep listening and **I** will bring you help as needed. All of **Our Walk** is centered in **Words of Truth**. Words of **Truth** are worthless unless they are spread about. It is the spreading that is about to come. Just trust and have confidence that **I** am in charge and **We** are going some place soon! Review and re-read the worthwhile words as **I** give you. Remember, **We** are a **Team Growing!**

Yes, **Our S.O.N.** is going where **I** want it. Be of good courage keep going and you will see! All **We** are doing is very pleasing to **The Father** and **He** cares! Keep seeking in **My Bible**. There is more to reveal, in obedience victory is achieved. Keep seeking in **My Word, I** have more to reveal. It is in obedience victory is achieved! Only consistent trying brings true revelation. When pushing on **My** part brings obedience on your part then new understanding will flow. **Our Walk** never dies down or comes to an end, only bodies get tired and slow down, but be of good cheer you are about to see renewal and have new growth in many ways. Hear **My Word** to you this day and see the blessings released. No child of **Mine** works without proper pay and **I** always reward handsomely, so keep open and doing as **I** desire and wait for good things to transpire. Yes, **We** are having a wonderful **walk** and yet **our** path has barely been shown to you.

OUR TRUTH

Never doubt, never part, only go on in **Truth** to see **Truth** flow out! All **We** do only grows as **We walk** hand in hand. Keep **Our Truth** dear to your heart for from there **We** formed **Our Path** and made **Our Start**. The things of the **Spirit** are truly a mystery to man, but revelation comes and understanding **will Stand**. Keep seeking and hope ever alive for on those things hang many a life. You may give **Me** a little, but **I** regard it as much, and you may never know why, for man lacks knowledge of such **Love** because it is **still** in its infancy! All of **Our Time** in the past has only been creating a place for **Our Future** to take off.

Yes, **Our** ongoing is only the unfolding of **Our Tale of Forever**! All any man does is leave the history of his **walk**. Some **walks** only crumble into worthless dust, but others build a forever castle of **Great Worth**! A place of **Always Remembered**. Few will build as **I** call for but many try. It is with great effort that **I** create ongoing lives of paths worth walking! Every child of **Mine** should wake up sooner, and work harder to find **Me**, then be more delighted about what **I Seek and Desire**. But that is **My** dream. How few even do a little bit. Every so often someone turns up and surprises **Me** by their attention paid to **My Desires**. These few Bless **My Heart**!

OUR TIME

Each of **Our** attempts to do must always come through the ways of this world, this is the trial of the flesh to test your **Spirit**. Have peace about your **walk**, **I** know all about it. Keep always the desire **I** put in your heart foremost, and then **I** can help work out your daily **walk**. Keep **Me** always by your side knowing then that **We are Winners**! All that you can do, **Do**! Let all else flow with the time. Only the things you accomplish for **Me** will ever count anyway! Let all of **Our Time** be sincere, and all the rest will be received with understanding. This **walk** is not finished yet and its success or failure is still in your hands. Keep always alert to **My Desires**, then **I'm** responsible for what transpires!

Remember, **We are a Team** working the works of **Him** who made this world and all that's in it. Keep **Our Goal** always in mind for then **The Father** is pleased. Let every day become **Father Pleasing**! Sometimes things seem upsetting that are only your imagination. Keep close to **Me** always, and forgetting the things of the world come into **Our Place** and rest. Yet a little while and **We** will have the time and rest of **My Promises**. Keep closer and closer as the times go by, and watch and wait expecting, then you'll see. Yes, this world and its people are changing. The great separation is occurring and **My People** are coming out. Pray more for them. These are to be times of **Doing for Me**, and by that **I** will know who **I** can trust forever! Just know and tell these things I am putting before you and fill **My** need in this area. Trust just a little time more, then **Our Work** will have its time!

MY WILL AND WAY

Keep the cares of this world always at a distance for they are inevitabley upsetting and eventually untrue! Draw closer into **My** work for you and **We** will prove the path **I'm** leading you on. Only

My Will and Way are to prove what's right. Keep drawing closer and closer, listening more and more for **We** are going on a good path to help many. Have no doubts and certainly no fear. For **The Father** is pleased with your **walk** with **Us**, especially when you keep always listening and drawing closer until **I** catch **My** dear ones away! Am **I** not slowly showing you **My S.O.N.** and revealing to you **My Purpose** for its disclosure? All of this will become quite reasonable and much clearer as **We** go along. This is dear to the **Father's Heart** and **He** watches over all **We** are doing! Isn't it interesting as more and more is disclosed?

What a good **walk We** are having by keeping this contact alive and growing. **Our Walk** in this opening of **S.O.N.** will only grow and open up new avenues of increasing interest. **The Father** is ready to tell more as this story expands in scope. **My Sea** has **Eternity** as its only witness up to now, but with the soon breaking forth of **My Bride** the **New** is being expanded.

Only in the **Spirit** can all be shown through times exposure, but now an opening picture may be exposed to believers of worth! Not all children or anyone will open their curiosity to such **Truth**, and they need have no interest in all **I** have! Eternity is long enough for all to grow and know. Right now the children who are **Truth Seekers** are the children to be rewarded and encouraged in all **We** desire to show.

The cross section of the children of the world is also as the cross section of heaven will be. Great differences and great ranges of desires, great ranges of dreams and hopes, as people are on earth so will that similarity be in Heaven. There will be no such thing as **Boring Sameness**. Seeking, searching with all your heart becomes saving grace from the start.

BECAUSE OF LOVE

THERE IS A PATH
THAT LEADS MEN UP,
HE HAS A CLIMB TO TAKE.

HE'LL NEED SOME HELP,
THE BIBLE GUIDES,
EXPOSING TRAILS OF FAKE.

CALL ON JESUS
HE'LL LEAD YOU TRUE,
NO FALSE STEP TO MAKE.

BECAUSE OF LOVE
HE'LL SEE YOU THROUGH,
IN YOU HE HAS A STAKE.

CHAPTER SEVEN

True Truth Seekers

Keep listening, reading the **Bible**, and drawing closer, this is the path to increasing **Oneness** which is the **Father's Goal** for all of **His** loved ones! Let **My Words** continue to flow into and out of your heart for this is for this time, a blessing required. **All Truth** has never been exposed and never will be because **All Truth is the Father Himself**! On the other hand **God's Truth** will never stop flowing to and through **His** loved ones. **Only Truth** growing keeps life worth living. **Truth** is the essence of **God's Life** manifested in all ways for **His Children**.

See why **I** make so much of **Truth**? See why Truth is so precious? See why Satan hides from Truth? See why **I** seek only **True Truth Seekers**, only they are men after **God's Heart**! See why **I** say love **Truth**, seek **Truth** with all your heart! See how **My Children** grow when they search for and find more and more **Truth**? See now the importance of all **Truth flowing in LOVE**, through **LOVE**, and with **LOVE**?

Let this day begin a **New Walk** in **New Ways**, and **Only** by recognizing your steps of growth will you know you are even growing? You must make agreement to finalize such a thing, *say it, give it attention to make it real, yes claim it*! Make sure of your way as **We** go! Looking back remembering where you used to be helps you realize the **True Path** of growth you have been on. Come into this kind of agreement on earth and then **We**, in **Heaven**, have something to agree with you about. This making **Real** what you are doing on earth is necessary; if you don't know its real then maybe it isn't!

You are standing before **The Doorway to Eternity** and waiting for this great time of entry. Keep making your position real in your hearts and in your minds. In the flesh this reality is still to be, but in the **Spirit** is where you are going. Yes there is just before you this **Great CHANGE in the Spirit Realm of** your **New Home**, and in your **Glorious New Spiritual Bodies**!

GUARDIAN ANGEL

Dear ones, to rise day by day early in the morning to be with **Me** will bring you to a place that is close to **My Heart**, and **I** wish to tell you so! Only this closer **walk** into **The Truth I** bring you will complete your place with **Me**. So many dear ones can never bring themselves to **Me** as they should. This is **The Self** still controlling, that should not be! Coming before **Me** daily in the quiet of the morning does much more than you ever have known or believed.

Yes, it gives your **Guardian Angels** much encouragement and draws them closer in fellowship as they watch over you. It tells them that there is truly a growing **love** between **Us** and you know it! This is part of the mystery to them of what and why **The Father** is so interested in you. [*Ephesians 3:10*] The actual living out in the flesh of your **Walk In The Spirit** is a mystery to them. Just believe to achieve by your attention given each morning, and then **I** can direct your footsteps into your final place with **Me**.

MY BLESSINGS

This rising early and being with **Me** is truly a path directed for **Blessing** upon **Blessing**. The timing of **The Blessings** is left up to **Me**. It is this waiting that proves the type, kind, and timing of **The Blessing. Blessings** are so varied that speculation seldom proves correct. **I** seek to fashion these blessings that become on going, consistently flowing, and in many cases endless kinds of blessings. When **I** fashion these blessings they are truly **Blessings to be Most Desired**. Not just a present to be unwrapped but a mantle to be worn, or a walk to be sustained! **My Blessings** are from **Heavenly** sources not earthly only blessings. **My Children** can not earn these kinds of blessings. They are unique and special, — **Made especially for My Children** kinds of blessings. I bring this word to you to encourage you and others that you relate this to. **My Blessings** are to be much desired!

The Truth these days has many distractions, but **My Word Stands Forever**. Stray not from **My Word** for it is the perfect discerner of **Truth** forever. Man himself has little or no truth of his own origin. Those who stray from **My Truth** are walking paths of quick disposal. Yes, **I** harbor no forgiveness for those who having **My Truth** then stray from it to follow their own beliefs. Led by self and Satan they will find little satisfaction before **My Court**! Follow always **My Bible** and seek only **Me** as the interpreter for **I** will never fail the **True Truth Seekers**! Yes, those of this world today who are acting as their own interpreter will find no peace and comfort at their conclusion. Draw closer to **Me** seeking **My Truth**, as **My Bible** declares, is the most safe passage for **My** children.

Our work must go on, to be faithful means all of the time! Only by steady work will all of this, **Our Task**, be accomplished. Don't let feelings rule, let **Spirit** be in charge, then your way will be sure!

Yes, every day now counts for something. For **Us** and for **The Father's Task**. Do not take all of this so lightly! It has much greater worth than what you are assigning to it. Only more will be revealed as more progress is shown. Keep all of this that **We** are doing on your front burner!

Let your day by day **walk** continue to grow in importance in **My Work** and so **We** will have great success. This book about **My S.O.N.** is truly rich in information and data **I** wish to present to **My Children. I** know how different this is, but isn't it increasingly interesting? Yes, let's keep it open and flowing and going. Yes, its going somewhere **I Desire**! There are places to go with this data and it will bless many believers. I'm letting **My Truth** flow in new areas because **My Children** need new encouraging. Just let patience be your guide because much needed encouragement will come out of this **Last Book**. These are **End Time Blessings** to be released for **MY Purposes** to be fulfilled! Do not be misled by anything but be led as **I** give directions!

Our journey continues into unknown realms, but not without security, safety, and always **Loving** care. As much as **I** am releasing through this way, **I** still have little to say about so huge a subject! It truly will take all of the countless ages and times that **I** have set for **My Family** to grow and move in **Our Forever**. When you consider **Forever or Eternal** as a place of all time events then the numerical system of man becomes a worthless tool of explanation! What an immense change for **Humans** when they **truly** enter **Eternal Life** with all of its ever-ongoing newness! Come **My** dear ones and prepare yourselves for a **Trip of Forever** with **Me** as your loving guide and trusted **Father**. Enhance this day, and all the rest of your days on earth, by growing close every day **Now with Me**!

The writing still goes on little-by-little until the small becomes the large! Yes, all of these words **We** write will grow and expand and bring forth a **New World** of meanings in which **The Father** will take great pride and interest. Surely all this will find a purpose and place of worth. All work brought out through man by **God** will be the **fruit of great value** as its purpose becomes clear in the minds of man. No **work** by **The Father** ever lays by the wayside to wither and die without purpose or use!

It is in the unfolding of **God's Purpose** that man's life, use, and time shows its **true** value. All things work together to satisfy the will of **Him** who creates and builds. A baby's manhood is never revealed until the life started has developed and grown. **Time** must serve the purpose of **Times Creator**! A scroll is just a roll of paper until the unrolling reveals all that is hidden inside. So the **works** of **The Father** must wait the slow unrolling of this **scroll** of **works** unfolding!

God is Good, God is Love and **His Love** abideth forever. You are **His Children**, the focus of **His Love**. **He** has given you free will to choose, to choose **His Way** or Satan's way. Life or death, and the world's way can be compelling but **His Way [God's Way]** brings lasting joy and peace. Know **His Word** and **His Directions** for your life and **His Promises** for you. Keep them close to your heart. Speak them often that they may make a lasting impression on your mind. Remember the mind is the battleground. If you dwell in the presence of **The Lord** your mind will be stayed on **Me**. Let **My** peace enfold you and **walk** with **Me** all the days of your life.

Keep faithful to this **Our Work** of **Now** for it is much desired by **The Father**. Never give less attention than is now being given for as **I** have said here before *"These written words are close to God's heart."* **Truly** this is to become a written work most desired! The only **Truth** is the **Ongoing Truth** a **Truth** that flows as **God Desires**. Have no doubts about **Our Walk or Our Work**! Keep **true** to this **work** and **I** will be **true** to it! Keep loyal to it and watch it flow and grow! What **We** do is what is to be done! **Our Walk** expands into more and more as **My Promises** have said already.

How else is **Truth for this Time** to be opened unless someone listens and cares? Keep open as long as **I** am giving words that flow. It is by your achieving by believing that **I** am relieving the weight of **The Father's Desires**.

The world is in darkness, but **I Am The Light**. Partake of **Me** and take of **My Light** that you may bring **Light** into the world. There is no **Light** except through the **Lord and Savior Jesus**. **His Love and Grace** shed upon **His** people bring **Light** to a sad world. **God is Love** and **His Love** has been given to you in the **Holy Spirit.** You are to share this gift of **Love** with others that they may know **Jesus** and turn their world from darkness to **Light**. Let **Love** cover all your actions and you will be **walking** in righteousness. When you **Love God** and **Love** others you are covered by **His Grace** and you sin not. You are always in **His** perfect will when **Love** directs your path.

Our closeness is to be a closeness never fully understood by men. **Our** closeness is to be just as **Jesus** is with **The Father**, as are all the **Sons of God**. This has been shown you in **My Word**. Do not let **The Truth** of it be lost or diminshed, This is Satan's desire. Do **I** not say you are seated at **My** right hand with Jesus? There are **Truths** that men are still blinded to because of man's unbelief, but these things should not be! As **I** have already said **My** children are **My Sons and Daughters** now and always. It is time for **Truth** to flow freely. Yes, freely, freely you have received freely freely give!

"The Lord is good, His mercy endureth forever." **God** hates sin and cannot look upon it. **His** wrath is on the sin in the world. However **He** has a forgiving **Heart** and will forgive sin if a sinner repents and asks for forgiveness. Stay close to **The Father** and **His** goodness. Keep your eyes on **Jesus** and **Do** have the mind of **Christ**, so that you will not be tempted. You have been given free will, choose wisely which path you will take. **Walk in the Light** and shun the darkness. **Let His Love and Peace** be your shield, your protection.

Wrap yourself in the joy of the **Lord** and you may draw others into **His Kingdom**.

Oh, how **I** desire **My** dear ones to awaken to all **Truth** that **I** have individually for each one. How quickly **Our Work** would be done and **Our Love** would grow unrestrained! Come all who hear this, **My Call** for all **I Love**, hear **My Heart's Desire** for **Our Walk** together. **I** have so much more **Truth** to give than **My** children ever imagined, yet **I** am restrained by **The Father** who has set the **Rules of Love I** must move in.

Only **The Path of God flows in His Truth and Way**; none other will be allowed, all is to be done in **Truth, Time, Testimony**, and **Testing! The Father's Plan** keeps **Our Eternity** safe forever, this is **His** great concern for **His Forever** with **Us**. This word should carry to you **love** most impressive, because it shows how carefully **Our Father** watches over all **He** is bringing to **Us**, and also bringing **Us** through to **Him! Love's Walk into Forever** has many obstacles and safeguards, but **His Hand of Love Guides All!**

"Be still and know that I am God." In Thy presence is fullness of joy, at thy right hand there are pleasures forever more." **My Children** live in **My Presence**. Live in the stillness so **I** can reach you. Surround yourselves with **My Peace** so **I Am** not blocked and unable to reach you. That **Peace** that passes understanding filters out sin, and the evil of the world, allowing **My Truth** and **Love** to fill your being. Cast out all negative thinking, change all wrong thoughts into **My** thoughts of love, peace, and joy. Release the fruit of the **Holy Spirit** into your life and truly know **I Am God!**

There are many assaults coming against **My** children, but **I** overcome them all. Keep drawing closer and closer as **I** give you time because **We are Victorious** over all the enemy throws **Our Way**. Grow stronger and stronger in faith day by day because **Faith is The Armor of The Lord!** Your **faith** in **My Word** and **Way** will pave all your streets with gold. **Believing Faith** paves streets of gold as **My Children walk** in the paths I have prepared and set before them. **My True Believers** will **walk** on water and then float in the air. Have **I** not already shown you your way?

"You have been redeemed by the blood of the lamb." You must choose this redemption and **Jesus Christ** who made it all possible. Continue to remind yourselves you have been redeemed and are forgiven. You are **truly** a **Child of God**, joint-heirs with **Jesus**. Forever have a heart filled with gratitude for this blessing. **Walk** daily being led by the **Holy Spirit** in you. **He** will show you **The Way** and will enable you to do all things. *"I can do all things through Christ which strengtheneth me."* Let **My Word** be the light that shows **The Way**. *"Thy word is a lamp unto my feet, and a light unto my path."* Think on this!

When **We** meet each morning you should bring your hopes and dreams. For only when **We Are One** in purpose can **Our Purposes** be fulfilled! It is important for you to express the where and what you desire to be, and then I can come into agreement. Even better is it when I express My Desires and **Will and Way**! You see growth in **Our Kingdom** is just such a place! A place where each express-es his personal wishes, hopes, desires, and then through agreement and understanding **We** are able to satisfy perfectly all that has been spoken and expressed.

This is the desired **way** of **Our Future** perfection as creation opens and flows into the vast places of the future intent! Those who learn and practice it now will be the forerunners of future growth! Am **I** opening reasonable and workable directions that are understand-able? It is in clear speaking and openness or purpose that all the delights of your future can be opened and displayed. Come now and learn **My Ways**, this will enable your quick promotion!

Take things as they come and handle them one at a time. In peace and patience determine what the **Holy Spirit** is telling you to do. **Listen** to the still soft voice of the **Holy Spirit**, because in **Him** is **The Wisdom of God**. **The Holy Spirit** is **All God**, "Given to You." It is up to you to release **The blessing**, and the fruit **He** has for you into your life. In peace be open for the direction **He** is showing you. Treat every situation with **Love** as a desire to do **God's Will**. Put self aside as it may become a stumbling block. *"Thy will be done in me and through me, oh Lord my strength and my redeemer."* Do let these words determine your attitude. Walk always in **My Presence** and **The Way** will be made clear.

The reviewing of **This Word** should set your purpose with **Me** on a **Solid Rock**! Do not let this pass by, for by lack of attention many a jewel is lost again in rocks and dirt! Stay more alert to the **Purpose** behind what **We** are doing and then **I** can guide your way more fruitfully! Only by always staying alert to what's happening can proper instructions be given. There is so much in what **We** are writing about that continuity is easy to lose. Stay focused as **I** try to keep **Us** on the path **The Father** is setting, **I** know too much can dull down enthusiam, so keep open to changes, explanations, and more instructions!

 As **I** am trying to keep **Our Story** open and clear, remember **Our Purpose** is to reveal **The Plan** and **Places** that **Our Father** has prepared or has in preparation for all of **His Children**. Little has been said about Israel, the Nations, the Angels and the Bride, all have their separate growth stories to be told, but right now **We** are concerned only with those involved in **The Rapture** and their places of **Beyond**.

"Call unto me and I will answer thee, and shew thee great and mighty things which thou knowest not." Call unto **Me** in all things for **I** desire to show you a better way. There is man's way and **My Ways**. **My Ways** always work together for good. In **My Love** for you **I** have prepared a **Special Path** just for you. You are free to

choose, I say, "choose **The Way of The Lord**." **Walk** in right-eousness and **My Way** will open up to you. **Walk** in **The Light** so no darkness can come upon you. In doing so I will always be with you, covering you with **My Love**!

It is the attraction to many things that causes **My** children to go astray from **Me**. In these times now, I try to explain this great necessity during these very last days! Come now doesn't this that you are reading have the ring of reality to it? I will release great growth to all who awaken to this **Truth**, and draw all their attention to their **Walk With Me**. Come now, I am speaking a great moving **Truth** to be obeyed! **I Will** take extra care with each obedient one who hearing this **Truth** obeys as best as they can! I say again **To the best of their ability**. I do not desire that this word I bring just lay dormant, but I do desire it to be broadcast about! Take consideration of **All that I Say**, but more so to words like this!

In winter, it is the dormant time, let it be so with your soul and **Spirit**. Let this be a quiet time in **The Lord** to grow **Spiritually**. **Now** you are to wait upon **The Lord** for truly **He** is doing great things. You must believe and trust that growth is taking place. **God** is working in your life, step back and let **Him** have **His Way. His Plan** is being performed in you, allow it to take place. *"Be still and know that I am God."* **The Holy Spirit** is releasing the fruit of love, peace, and joy into your life as you let go and let **God**. It must not be any of your work or plans, but rely totally on the **Lord** to develop in your being the plan **He** has for you.

Yet another day, what will you make of it? Or what will it make of you? When **I Am** with you will you let **Me** "Make Your Day?" Your **walk** only gets you someplace when **I'm Leading**! If I look back often will I always see you there? This is not the place **I'm** drawing you to, not a place in back of **Me** but along side of **Me**, make this desire of **Mine** your desire. Let it grow until all you do will be "What **We** are doing!" **I am** big enough to do this for every child of **Mine**. How else can they all find their **True Abode** unless they willingly stick to **My Purposes** for them? **Our Books** are for **My Children's Growth** and in that purpose they will find its place. Keep **My S.O.N.** growing in **My Truth** and **Purpose** for it is becoming a blessing to **Me**! May this trickle of **Truth** bring *Showers of Blessings*!

"Be aglow and burning with the Spirit." Are the Father's Words to you. Let there be a glow about you, a light coming from the inside out. **God is Love**, **God is Light** and **He** will impart this **Love** and **Light** to **His Children** who are receptive! As your heart is filled with **His Love**, the **Light** will shine forth from you. It will be a beacon of **God's Love** to others. Show forth **His Love**; **talk** the **talk** and **walk** of **True Love** one to another. Be consistent, gentle, tender hearted and understanding to all. Show forth the meekness that is a fruit of the **Holy Spirit** released into your life. You are to be a **True** representative of **Jesus** and **His Love**. Put self aside and abide in **Me** and **I** will direct your path of **Love**!

Time drives **Me** and **My Children** in these end times, but never believe that **I Am** not in charge. Only those who **walk** with **Me**, enjoying the path **I** lead them on, will ever understand and give full attention as **I** direct. Keep these days close to your heart as you **walk** and **abide** in **My Desires** and **Will** for you. It is in this attitude of obedience that you pave your **Streets of Gold**. Have no doubts EVER for that is rebuke of **My Ways** *that I will not harbor or accept*!

True Believers are never led astray or turn from **Our Way**! It is with this winning attitude **I** can build **Castles I Desire**. Always know to whom you belong and where **We** are going and what **We** are doing. Am **I** not leading, and do you truly follow in the things **I** ask? Revelation Knowledge is My Way of teaching, leading and guiding in these end times, because man's way is fast embracing the confusion of evil worldly ways. Soon there will be little hope for their choice is all consuming. Let this open eyes to how devastating evil has become!

Trust in **Me** to see you through by putting your life in **My Hands** and **I** will make all things possible. Rest when you are to rest, work when there is work to be done. Lean on **Me** for together **We** can do all things. **My Word** is **True**, *"I can do all things through Christ who strengtheneth me."* and *"But my God shall supply all my needs according to His riches in Glory by Christ Jesus."* Keep your eyes on **Me** and not on the problem at hand for **I am** your strength and **I** will sustain you.

I walk together with all **My Children, We** are not done yet! Keep on with the work **I've** given you for it is a blessing to **My Heart**, stay with it and **I** will make it a blessing to many! It is in the doing that **My Children** bless **Me**, and all their **Doings** that they do for **My Sake** pleases **Me**, and **I** watch over all that **My Children** devote themselves to. Just know and believe how close **We** are to **Our Great Meeting**. Keep telling all who you can! Keep a day of rest for **Glorifying the Lord**. Know that the work I began **I** shall perform!

Be **My** willing vessel and **I** will lead you into a **heavenly walk** with **Me**. Forget self and focus on your **Lord** and **Savior, Jesus**. Remember what **He** has done for you and let your thanksgiving burst forth in praises and worship. Be ye kind and loving one to another as **I** have **loved** you. For **I Am Love** and **My Love** has been imparted to you. Share **love** with all others as **I** have commanded. In this there is joy for evermore!

Yes, this **walk** is still the only way to go for now. Keep always close in this same manner until change is so obvious that it just flows! Never be discouraged, it is **The walk** that is **Your Victory** not any **Event**! Just keep up the Walk of Truth and the **Way of Truth** will prove its self! Knowing the **way** you're going all of the time isn't

Our Purpose, it is just in **The Walk** that purpose is fulfilled to **My Desires**! Enjoy each day with the victory and you are attaining, not in any single celebration! As **I** reveal to you the things on **My Heart, We** can together enjoy each small attainment! Ongoing is life's victory!

Lift up your heads and know that your strength and your joy comes from **The Lord**. Do not look to any earthly thing to fulfill your being. Let your love, your prayer, praise, and worship be the connection that binds **Us** together. Persevere under all trials and problems. Going through them with **My Covering** and **I** will lift you up. In every test know that **I Am** with you. Lean on **Me**, "*Wait upon the Lord and He shall renew your strength.*" Be filled with the peace that passeth understanding in all things for **I** am with you. Keep pressing forward toward the goal **I** have planned for you!

THE PATH THAT'S SURE

FIND IN ME A PLACE TO HIDE
KNOWING I'M ALWAYS BY YOUR SIDE.
MY LOVE LIKE WARM BLANKETS COVERING
SENDS BLESSINGS ABOUT AS DOVES HOVERING.

PEACE OF HEART IS YOUR SURE PLACE,
KEEPING YOU FROM EARTH'S FAST PACE.
STAY ON MY PATH, IT'S TRUE AND SURE,
KNOW YOU'RE SAFE FROM THINGS THAT WERE.

RISING EARLY WITH ME MEETING,
IN FELLOWSHIP THE SONSHINE GREETING.
LET OUR LOVE FLOW OUT EACH DAY
KNOWING OTHERS HAVE FOUND THE WAY.

CHAPTER EIGHT

Introducing
The Speaking Spirit

It is necessary to insert at this time and place, in this **Book of My Sea Of Nothing**, *a teaching of great importance* to those who believe in what has been revealed up to this point. It is **My Desire** that every **Child of Mine** be so instructed that they will be led, directed, taught and guided by **My Spirit**. It is necessary that all come to the same place **Jesus** came to on **His Walk** in the flesh. That is to the position that **He Did Nothing** except what **I Told Him** to do. **I** give **The Speaking Spirit** to **My** willing workers. Let **The Speaking Spirit** be present now in obedience to **The Father's Will**. It is necessary for this opening of **Truth** to flow freely to **My Listening Ones**. **Only Truth Flowing** will bring change required to cause **The Gathering Blessings** to flow.

Only in **Truth** of **My Purpose** can this mighty move take place in this time now opening, no true child will be missed, and every false child will be exposed. As this force of gathering takes place, **We** will experience a newness coming upon all of the **Elect** of this age. No instant change takes place but a refreshing **Washing of the Word** will bring understanding to the chosen ones. Each will move in unison of **My Purpose**. Obedience is the **Flow of Love** moving to serve **My Desire**. **My Way** will have **Love's Hand** covering every move in perfection of purpose and timing, and all **Truth** needed will be made apparent to everyone of perfection. Take this hint of **Truth Flowing** as the preliminary opening phase that is coming.

Only as **My Children** gather together in unity can **My Truth** impact them as it should. In fellowship of agreement you will find **My Directions** given freely. By and through **My Speaking Spirit** will **My** end time lessons of **Truth** be spread causing gathering of **Truth** that exposes **My** Desires! **All Children** should come to this way of end time growth. The **Way of Spirit** teaching of **Guidance** and **Truth** is for the last days of growing into **Spirit Perfection**! I will grant the **Speaking Spirit** to all who open their hearts to **Me**. All of these following scriptures give understanding about **The Speaking Spirit**. Adam was a **Speaking Spirit**, and to Israel He was called "A Speaking Spirit," that gave to **Me** a companion **I** could converse with readily.

I Kings 19:12,13 tell of **My** first gift to man of **My Speaking Spirit**, before that **I** spoke face to face with those whom **I** desired, or in other ways at different times. This gift **I** gave to others in the **Old and New Testament**. The **Speaking Spirit** is **Jesus** or **Myself** speaking to whomsoever **We** desire as friends, and enjoying **Ourselves** as **We** wish as **We** indwell them. Study the following scriptures to find answers that satisfy. *Deut. 4:33, Deut. 5:4, 2 Chron. 36:12, Eze. 43:5-7, Acts 26:14, II Cor. 13:3.* **Truth** is a flowing stream most children don't want to dip into. Keep close track and attention to the words shown to you for there is the place **I** can show others the worth of what you are doing [Reading this work]. **Our Work** must break out in and flow in **The Truth I Am** always speaking of. Keep this kind of **Truth** always before you for here is the crux of **Our Work**! It is **My Desire** that **My Words** here be made known and properly respected. **We** will find outlets of worth for these **truths** to be made known and shown proper respect! **Truth** doesn't need proving except to unbelievers! **My Children** who listen and receive **Truth** are the ones that **I** desire to feed that **I** may be shown just who they are and where **I** can use them. All of this is to be for the purpose of lifting these ones higher as they respond and show their worth!

You have the mind of **Christ** within you. It is in the **Holy Spirit**, your gift from **God** when you accepted **Jesus** as your **Lord** and **Savior**. **The Holy Spirit** within is your helper, your comforter, **He** has blessings untold stored up for you. Oh **My Children** open up your hearts and release these blessings from **Me** into your hearts and into your lives. **I** have gifts of love, peace, joy, patience, gentleness and goodness, gifts of faith, meekness and self control stored up for you in **My** precious **Holy Spirit**, grow into these blessings. Allow them to come into your being and help you become the person **I** have planned for you to be. Grow **Spiritually** daily by letting go and letting **God, The Holy Spirit,** be the leader in your life. *"As many as are led by the Spirit of God, they are the sons of God."* Release **My Power** into your life and receive all the blessings **I** have for you.

Share what **I** have given you with others. Do not store up the blessings but pass them on so that all **My Children** may be blessed. *"My God shall supply all your needs according to His riches in glory by Christ Jesus."* **Walk** fully convinced that **I** will perform **My Words** and all your needs and desires will be fulfilled. Walk in **My Mercy** and **My Love** for you are **My Beloved** children. Be still and know that **I Am God** when the cares of the world surround you. **Walk** and have your being in **My Presence**. Lean on **Me** for **I Am** your strength forever. This day by day way of growing closer is the best way for **Us** to become **One.**

Why doesn't this all come about sooner or faster or easier? **The Father** is dealing with a pure **Eternity**, and there is only one way for that to come about safely, and that is why there is a 7 year plan [seven thousand years]. All growth is a cutting down and weeding out of every possible hindrance to a perfect **Forever**. It is **love** of that purpose that drives every cautious step being taken. The growth of a pure **Family of God** is the only way for **The Father's** satisfaction to be complete. The final seal of this guarantee is **His** coming into every child chosen and abiding in them forever! What a perfect path of completion this is!

You have been cleansed. You have been freed from sin and the darkness in your soul by the cleansing blood of **Jesus, My Son!** That is **My Gift** to you when you received **Jesus** into your life as **Lord and Savior**. Now allow **Jesus** and the **Holy Spirit** to do the work that has been assigned to lift you up. You must desire to **walk** with **Me** and live in **My Presence**. Let **My Love** fill you constantly and overflow to touch all others around you. By prayer, worship, and praise always keep **Our** connection intact. **I Am** always with you, do not turn from **Me** for **I Am** your strength and peace and your source of **All Things**!

When **My Voice** is questioned it is only the questioner that will come under scrutiny! Let the doubters have their way and say, for they will only be condemning themselves by their words. All **My Believers I** will open their ears to know **My Truth** when spoken. Never fear for then Satan is near! **Truth** will always prove itself.

Keep back only that which **I** caution you to hold back! **Our Work** will be exposed by **Me** at the proper times and places when it proves necessary. When **I** give release **Truth** will flow in acceptable ways even new believers will hear and understand. **Truth** will leap barriers and **I** will bring **My Pleasures** into being. Much is yet to flow with this ending just before you. Great will be **Our Harvest** as released **Truth** brings the last loved ones into their places. All is done! All is to be, no force can stop it, and then this closing is closed!

Our Work is some inspiration, some perspiration, **but mostly obedient listening**. Let desire continue for the prize is only at the end. I make the start and **I** make the end. It's all in the **walking** it that proves the worth. This doesn't mean its not fun and worth while during the trip. Take each day for what it is, just another step to where you are going.

Always keep **Our Goal** in sight, letting **Dreams**, **Hopes** and **Desires** build on all that transpires. Let **Trust** build walls of security all around you as time rolls out its ups and downs. It's all in **Faith** and **Believing** that brings things worth achieving, while testing and trials hardens the soul's **Truth Walk**. Just build confidence in where **I'm** taking you knowing **I'm** always along by your side. **Our Goal** does not come to a great climax and then end, you'll always find many more things intriguing just around the bend.

Our Way is not down a straight, long road, but it is found to be an always enjoyable trip with many pleasant hills and valleys filled with loving people, scenes, and adventures. **Our Walk** always has purposes to be fulfilled and advantages to be gained! Yes all **My Children** shall come around to know **Me** as **Father**, and **Jesus** as **Teacher**, that is as you come to believe.

This is the **Path of Truth** that all **My Children** must come to! All your thoughts, hopes, and cares must finally come to this place of knowing **My Family** is **All My Children**, and they are brothers and sisters in and through **Christ** who opened heaven's doors to **My Forever** for them. **All Truth** comes as all barriers are broken down in each life. Yes each **True Child of Mine** must travel **Truth's Path of Victory**! This is **True Teaching** that is traveling on **The Way**!

TRUTH'S PATH

IT'S ONLY IN AN OPEN HEART
I CAN PLACE TRUTH TO START.
NEVER BELIEVE SELF CAN ACHIEVE,
WITHOUT MY TRUTH YOU'LL GRIEVE.

THE PATH IS FOR TRUE TRUTH SEEKERS,
NOT FOR LOST OR CASUAL PEEKERS.
BRING YOUR TRUST TO TRUTH IN FAITH,
THEN I CAN GIVE SAVING GRACE.

FIND A HEART CHANGE, DO IT NOW,
I'LL GIVE YOU TRUTH SHOWING HOW.
THE GOAL TO SEEK IS TRUTH REFINED,
AND I CAN SHOW MY TRUTH YOU'll FIND.

CHAPTER NINE

Time—Eternity's Segments

Time does move along faster than man realizes, but **My Children** know what **Time** is! **Time** is a most important subject for man to have total comprehension about. It is a gift for man to make him realize there is a **God**. It is set for man to have greater awareness of **My Works**. It is **Work** for man to wake up and study, for **I** hold all of **My Works** carefully in segments of eternity called **Time**. Yes **I** created **Time** as a calendar of sequence of **My Works**. **I** do nothing that is outside of a **Time Schedule**. **My** existence is ever ongoing and **I** have made **Time Segments** of great worthiness!

So **I** call man to take careful note of the **Time Places I** have called for man to have, and all the **Time Places I** have not ever revealed to man. So much is set before **My Children** when they are confronted with their **Creator of Time! Our Eternity** is made up of all kinds of segments **I** call **Time**. There is no set length, except as man knows **Time,** that is why a day is as 1000 years to **Me**. Come dear ones, this is but a small opening to **My Wonders in Time! I** have opened your eyes that you might relate to this story of **My S.O.N.** making it more believable! Yes that you know is **true**, and you can tell it is because the way seems right to you. This is the **Very End Times**, [for this age] and **My Children** can now be opened to more **Truth** about **My Times!** All that **We** have been doing will come to great purpose shortly. It is **Truth** telling that relates, that will help

My Children come to **Me** quickly. This is an **End Time's** blessing just before the catching away!

Glorify your **Heavenly Father** for **He** is worthy. Allow **His Glory** to penetrate your being, and live always in **His Presence**. **Walk** upright, strong in **The Lord**. When you are weak **He** is strong. **Truly**, *"The Joy of the Lord is your strength."* Lean on the **Lord** for from **Him** comes your life. Take **His Word** to heart, *"I can do all things through Christ which strengthens me."* Stand tall knowing you are a child of **God** and **He** is watching over you all the **Time** in **Love**. Be not consumed with self, but let **Jesus** into your life and self will slowly fade away in **Time**. **Jesus** is the **Light** of the world, let this **Light** invade your being and you can be an effective child of **God** doing **His Work** here on earth.

Rise up and **walk** with **Me. Today** especially live in **My Presence** and partake of **My Love**. Have joy in the birth of **My Son Jesus** who is your **Lord** and **Savior**. **He** has been sent from **Heaven** to free you from bondage, to cleanse you of all iniquities, to heal your infirmities and to cover you with **Love, Peace**, and **Joy. Rejoice** for **today** is a **Time of Salvation** through **Jesus**. Let all men choose **The Savior** sent from **God**. *"For God so loved the world that He gave His only begotten Son that whosoever believeth in Him should not perish, but have everlasting life." John 3:16* Celebrate the birth of **Your Lord** and **Savior**.

These days, during these **Times Now**, are going to mean more and more, so be ready as never before for greater activity than has been. We are going to move on in **Our Work** set by **The Father** so look forward to these coming **Times** with great anticipation. **I Am** moving things now as never before around you, and you will come to know what this **Time** spent with **Me** has come to mean in your lives. Keep drawing closer all of the **Time Now** for this will be the way of **Our Victory**. Believe for more and more and keep closer to **Me** than ever before! Use this **Time** to get more and more out of

The Bible and watch the **Blessings** develop! Keep drawing closer in **Our Walk** as these **Times** will bring more meaning all of the **Time**. Yes, let these **Times** be "Down Hill" travel.

My dear ones keep this constant pursuit of **Truth** ever before you and **We** will **walk** a great path of purpose together. All that seems right many times is man just missing the mark! See that you do not do so! Every **walk** of man picks up the unwanted bits of trash, it is important only how long they are carried! **Discard anything that has an appearance of such a thing! These** are **Times** that require a careful walk of **My Purposes**, dropping all self-pleasing that you can.

Jesus is the **Light** of the **World**. Partake of **Him**, fill your soul with **Jesus** and **He** will dispel the darkness from your life. *"Cast your cares on Him for He cares for you."* Lay aside the burden and worries of self and the world, and **walk** in a higher realm. You have been freed from sin, so live in this freedom, in the **Presence** of the **Lord. Now** is **The Time** to let joy fill you being, let peace that has been given to you reign and direct you. *"Peace I leave with you, My peace I give unto you; not as the world gives, give I unto you. Let not your heart be troubled, neither let it be afraid." John 14:27.*

Keep your thoughts on **Me**. For protection plead the **blood** of **Jesus** in **His Name** over your property and your family. In these **End Times** you need the protection of the **blood** of **Jesus** over your lives. Evil is fighting a desperate fight but, *"Greater is He that is in you than he that is in the world."* Stand firm against the devil and the evil around you. You have total protection covered in **Jesus' Blood**. Call on the **Name of Jesus** and plead **His blood** over your house and family. Let your **faith** rise and believe that **The Word** is true. *"They overcame him by the blood of the lamb, and by the word of their testimony."* Sin, temptation, sickness and disease, everything that comes from Satan is included in that. **Stand** fast in **faith**! The pursuit of **Truth** is a pathway no man should overlook. **My**

Bible, when properly read, makes this **Pursuit of Truth** of the greatest importance; yet how many of **My** servants talk, preach, or dwell on this pursuit? To keep **Truth** ever present is to follow **My Desires** to the fullest! So search for and continually seek after **Truth** in what **I** have said. Let your searching always stay on this path that **Truth** will lead you on. Let **My Talk** like this continually be your path of seeking **Truth**. **I'm** the end of all things in the flesh, only **Truth** "properly discerned" will lead you to **My Everlasting Arms**! The pursuit of **Truth** is a pathway no man should overlook.

Our Time is still growing and you have no idea where. It is in the **walking** each day and in **Its** reality that you slowly will come into **My Reality**.This is the **Time and Place** all of **My Children** should grow into, but they seldom search it out for themselves, and few of **My** learned ones spell it out for many. **I'm** explaining to you now things of worth, to be noted and acted upon! **I** never said **My Walk** was easy, but **I** have said, over and over, that it is very worthwhile with great big pay offs! As you grow to understand, try to relate this to those **I** bring before you! **Our Walk** together is for the purpose of spreading **The Truth to "Truth Seekers."** False listeners are many, but True Truth Seekers never turn away or give up, this is their **Time!**

The **Times** that are coming upon you are bringing to a **Climax** the work of **Jesus.** These days must come to an end, a completion, to this work in the **Body of Christ**. Where should all of this go? The end is **The Gathering** at the last of this age of the gentiles. Yes, and end must come or the **Glory of Jesus** will never be shown! In light of all of this shouldn't every effort be made now to bring into this closing **Time** every last child of **God**? This also includes drawing every seeking, believing child of **God** into the highest and best place they can achieve in the flesh. Yes? Then continue to study the lessons **We** have prepared for this purpose. Let each day now be set toward that goal!

This is to start your new **walk**, stay closer to **Me** and **We** will have a great **Time**. This day is to bring many more to **Our** table and **My Truth** will begin to flow. Only by **Our** working more closely all of the **Time** can **Truth** move as **I** desire. Yes, **We** are going somewhere, and you should just keep drawing closer. Give no thought to the things about you, that is just the way things are! Always keep calm for there will be many disappointments ahead, but look for **The Blessings** Only!

GOD'S SONGS FLOW

DO YOU HAVE A GOD SONG TO SING?
CAN YOUR HEART FEEL HIS HEART?
WILL HEAVEN'S JOY MAKE YOUR EARS RING?

YES, MY CHILDREN LEARN TO SEEK
SONGS OF HEAVEN TO PLEASURE EARTH
KNOWING THEY RING OUT TO GIVE MAN A PEEK

OF GLORIES OF GOD, AND MUSIC SO REAL,
THAT ALL GOD'S CHILDREN ARE MEANT TO HEAR
THE JOY OF HEAVEN, YES, HEAR AND FEEL!

SO BEND SPIRIT'S EAR SO YOU'LL KNOW
FROM HEAVEN WILL FLOW SONGS MAN HEARS
KNOWING GOD'S SONGS MAKE HIS LOVE FLOW.

CHAPTER TEN

A Window Opened

I will continue in **Truth, Direction, Blessings, and Ongoing** as **I** desire. **We** still have bridges to cross and words to be delivered, so keep ever drawing closer in this task! **Our Time** is just as **The Father Desires**, so never let your desires show in any strength, way, or purpose. Only what **The Father** desires is what **We** are searching for!

A TRUTH WALK IN LOVE

This Walk requires a drawing closer to The Father Now.
Keep Seeking in Silence, be encouraged in the doing.
Pray more about this than any time before.
Grow in confidence in this New Walk KNOWN!
This closer Walk is the cement holding more and more.
Believe for increase in Revelation Knowledge.
Let this Walk open Families to a closer bond in Love.
Let Families find togetherness from this Walk.
A pile of Glory is waiting to be discovered and SHOWN.

TRUTH

The pursuit of **Truth** is **My children's** true **Hope**. In this search lies all the power man will ever need to fulfill **My Word** for them. The **True Truth Seekers** seek only for the perfection of **My Son Jesus**. Yes this is the **Way** of all who seek to attain **My Will** and **Way**. They must come through the **Way of The Cross** and bear the stamp of perfection **I** gave **Jesus**. Tell **My children** to listen carefully and receive the **Truth** only **Jesus** can bring to them. They must learn to listen carefully in the still of the morning, and then **We** can gather and lead all to **Our Heavenly Home** together. Coming into **Oneness** is the **True Walk** of **My Purpose** for all of **My** dear ones. Teach, Lead and Guide all who will listen, heed and obey. The days are fewer than ever for all who would attain to **My Victory** for them. Spread this **Word**; tell all who listen and you will see **My Victory** unfold!

Truth is a path when researched always shows **My Work** in reality. It is a **walk**, difficult for mere man, but for **My Children My Light** shows the **Way**! Come lose the blindness of man Satan has put there, and know the light of **My Shinning Path**! **I** will open the seeking eyes, **I** will lead the willing hearts, **and I** will open doors of **Wonders** in **Truth** to all who has **My Spirit of Truth** indwelling them. This release only comes through the sincere, searching and seeking, efforts of opening the **Doors of My Way**. Release self and follow **My Heart** for you, then you will "**Know Me in Spirit** and soon in **Truth**."

Only persistent seeking after **My Truth** will any **Truth** be found. Remember doubting, questioning, wondering about, maybe, not knowing, will not bring anyone to the place of true release. This is the way of it; **Truth** is **Spiritual Reality** in the physical realm of material things. That is why new ideas just seem to come *all of a* *sudden*. It is **Truth** revealed from the **Spirit** to be manifested in the physical. Children born of **My Spirit** should show more of this than unsaved man, but many times **I** must use unsaved man because **My** children won't hold still long enough to be used properly. **I** must use minds which are more open to **My** deep **Truths** than they are to **Me!**

Let your **faith** increase for surely your **Father** is with you. **He** has promised to be with you always. **He** will never leave you, however you are free to **walk** with **Him** or to do your own thing. Choose the path **He** has set before you and truly *"All things will work together for good."* **God's Plan** is filled with your protection and **His** mighty Love, Peace, and Joy! **He** knows you and **He** knows what you need to grow **Spiritually**. Be as a small child, **He** will guide you into a closer **walk** with **Him**. **He** will open the **way** to a **Oneness** with **Him** and into **His World of Righteousness** and pure **Love**!

In this time **We** have together dwell more on nothing, it allows **Me** to bring what you need. This lesson is one few children understand as they should. It centers on **Trust** in **Me** for your needs. Only by your silent release can **I** bring you this growth needed. Growth is increasing your **Spiritual** awareness of **My** help. Nothing physical is apparent so it is missed. Your **Spiritual** growth is now your important next step. In patience all is accomplished. Your trip is "From" the flesh to the **Spirit. Silence** is the place of **Travel, Faith,** and **Trust** are your vehicles of movement. See how simple it really is when clear paths of **Truth** are opened?

DIRECTION

To find your proper place in the **Lord** is the purpose of these studies. Your way is to be given to you in your morning devotions with the **Lord**. Only the **Lord** will direct you as you seek a closer walk with **Him**. This approach is simple. Wake up early, meet with **Him** in silence, the length of time is your choosing, let the **Lord** guide you. As you sit in silence dwell on nothing, just listen and stay in this altitude of listening. The purpose is to draw you into a closer walk in **The Spirit**; you're seeking growth in **The Spirit**. Nothing apparent will be happening. [Remember you're still in the flesh, and this is growth in **The Spirit**.] This only happens as you believe and submit to **His** purpose for you. Next, spend time hearing from the **Lord God** and writing down what **He** has to say to you. Why write it down? If it is from the **Lord God of Heaven** speaking to you it should be important enough for you to write it down. Great growth will occur through your rereading as time goes by. **His Word** of **Truth** is always useful!

My children can only be drawn into the **walk** they should take by constantly being encouraged and talked along. Pray more about what **We** are trying to do and **I** will be released to be more help. As you can see **We** have begun a **new walk** as **I** have said. Yes more opportunities will open up and **We** will have more blessed times. Keep more open daily than you have been because only then can **We** grow closer for your growth. Keep this door open **now, Our** talks will expand and **Our** depth of new teachings will open up new and deeper **truths** of great worth at this time, never doubt how **I** will use these teachings. Only confidence building in what **We** are doing will continue this **walk**.

Let's make each day a day of remembrance! All **I** desire must be released sometime and why not **now**? Let **Our Walk** open up into more and more as **I** have promised. Only obedience comes from doing, and doing is what doers do! Not all things here are perfect, but until trying does its thing can anything be shown or proved or worthwhile? Let all doers lean on **Me**, and then **We** can pull together making the set mark achievable! Always **walk** with **Me** in all things, and then you will have all **The Comforter** can lead and guide you to and through. Only **Our Walk** together can prove anything!

This is the time for perseverance in your life. Resting in the **Lord** you will go forward. *"Be still and know that I am God."* You are part of a support system and necessary to **My Plan**. Gently and in patience go forth with a loving heart. Wait upon the **Lord** and **He** will renew your strength. **He** will lift you up! You have not because you ask not! Call upon the **Lord** in all things knowing He is a **loving God**.

He hears your prayers and is drawing you into a closer **walk** with **Him**. *"Trust in the Lord with all your heart, lean not on your own understanding. In all your ways acknowledge Him and He will direct your path."* **Our Walk** together is beginning to open new doors for many who will listen and pay attention. This **walk** is where you are to go and **I** am with you! It is only through your obedience that **I** can do anything, and **I** want to do more and more all the time! Keep your feet on the ground and **I'll** take you into **heaven's** far reaches!

Go about this day with peace and harmony in your soul. Rest in the **Lord** and wait upon **Him**. **He** will clear the way before you. Be in the **Word** constantly that you may be strengthened. Claim **His Words** as your own. **His** promises are for you. **Walk** confidently as a child of **God**, being lifted by the **Word**. See yourself in **His** presence for *"In thy presence is fullness of joy, at thy right hand there are pleasures forevermore."* Persevere through each circumstance knowing that the **Lord** is with you. **He** will see you through. Let **His Love, Peace and Joy**, so readily available, be your guiding light.

Our work must move on for time pushes **Us**. Keep open for more and more. All **Our** work will find its way so keep pushing a little all of the time! Keep open for more and more from **My Bible** for that is **My Way**! Just let the **Sea Flow** you will understand more and more as **We** grow together in this **walk!** Nothing is given easily or quickly, perseverance and patience must have their way. Keep on with what you are given here. Many of **My children** need stir-ring up, this is as things need to be, and should be! Only as **I** lead can **Our Way** be made sure!

Be filled with joy, the joy of the **Lord**, and all things will be doable. **God** will make a way. Go boldly forward and know that the **Lord** will sistain you in all your ways if you **walk** with **Him**, keeping your eyes on **Jesus**. Be strong in the **Spirit**, filled with power and strength of the **Lord.** *"I can do all things through Christ who stren-thens me."* Do not run ahead of the **Lord**, remember, *"They that wait upon the Lord shall renew their strength."* **I** would have you in **My Will** always.*"In My Presence is fullness of joy."* Live in this **Presence**!

BLESSINGS

Our door of opportunity is swinging open; do not try to guess where **We** are going! **I** can expand this only as **I** see fit. **My Plans** are ever **increasing**! Only a closer **walk** all the time is the bond that holds more and more. Believe for *increase* in children drawn together, *increase* in locations to gather together, **increase** in knowledge released, and new ideas of use shown. Only this **increase** in believing can bring on an expansion of interest and opportunities.

Give and it shall be given unto you. Be free to give as unto **The Lord** and **He** *shall supply your every need*! **Trust in the Lord** and **His Promises** to take care of you. **He** will **truly open** the windows of heaven and pour blessings upon you. Let your **faith** grow and receive what **God** has for you. **God's Love** is an **ever lasting bless-ing. His Power** comes when you receive this **Love** and become a clear channel to others. Do not limit anything by doubt. Keep open to **My Truths** in the **Bible** and in **Our quiet Times**. With more learning the things taught here, there will be more children grow-ing into **Truths**. This is to be opened up to families to bring a clos-er bond in **Love**, bringing a **new oneness** to their **walk**.

This time will be just right, for this will be a rapid move with many children involved! Do not doubt this move, only believe, for **now** this **door is opening**, and **now** believing will be on the increase. This is a new release around the **World. I** am not limited to some small groups, but every obedient child is being called for this is a last great explosion of **My Truth** breaking out. Seek out the hungry ones and feed them. Look for kindred souls seeking a **closer walk**. Spend more time **In The Silence** with **Me.** *This is most important for this word to be spread.*

Keep always seeking, because **I'm** always giving to those who keep seeking with hope in their heart. Never doubt, never demand, be always aware of who you are! Yes act as though **We** are **One,** believe **We** are **One,** for **Oneness** is the one goal all **My Children** should desire above all things! When you come to this action in belief, then **We** can do great things! It is only with the doers that **I** can draw out the desires of **My Heart in Truth**. Only **Truth** reveals more **Truth,** but only as belief is sure and true! Carefully watch over **My Words** for only they reveal **Our Oneness** in and through **Truth!** Be a **Truth Seeker, I Am Truth.**

Let the warmth of the sun stir the joy in your hearts. Do not lose the joy of the **Lord** for through this comes your strength. **Walk** in **My Presence** for **I** am leading you on a path that has been prepared for you. *"Thy word is a lamp unto your feet, a light unto your path,"* **I** would have you stay on track by the **Word** and the guidance of the **Holy Spirit**. Be at peace always. **My Word** tells you *"Thou will keep him perfect peace whose mind is stayed on thee."* Have the mind of Christ and be in **My perfect** peace always. Let the **joy** of the Lord be your **peace** and **strength.**

Keep drawing closer all of the time, you are pleasing to **Me!** Continue in **Our** pursuit of **Truth** yielding words as **I** give them. Only **true Truth Seekers** will ever find **Our Work** pleasing! **I** guide, lead, command, and control only from **Truths** high and honorable position! **My children** will all come to see, know, understand, and join **Us** in this, the only way to go! All **We** will ever do together will never depart from **My High Way of Truth! Children** of this world must grow to accept this **Way** for only those will ever know **The Everlasting Life** that **I** hold out now as a free gift to **all** of **My Believers**!

The Lord wants to give you a gentle heart, a kind and loving heart, always looking for the good in others. See in others what **God** sees in them. If you shine **the light** on the good the darkness will fade away. Let **His** presence determine your attitude. *"Seek ye first the kingdom of God and His righteousness, and all these things shall be added unto you."* Stand fast and be bold in the freedom you have received from your **Lord**. Be bold in meekness, in a quiet **Spirit**, reflecting the **light** that has been given you. Let the love and peace of **His** presence enfold your soul. In this manner you truly will be joint-heirs with **Jesus.**

Many are the distractions of the day, but this also is a test **I** bring. Who are **My** overcomers, who puts **Me** and **My Desires** first and foremost daily? **I** seek to know this, yes this is one thing **I'm** always looking for! Give careful thought each day, asking what does **My Lord** require or desire this day? Here is a test most fail. **I** am not trying to take away anything of your will and way, but **I** do carefully watch over all who are showing some concern for **My Desires** and **My Will** and **Way**!

To whom do you belong and to whose house will your desires take you? Am **I** too pushy? Well your time is growing shorter and shorter, what should your desires be doing for you? Always keep in mind who's you are, and to whom you belong. When you are properly obedient to these questions then **We** can do great things, even in this short flesh time that you have. **I** will never fail you, leave you or forsake you, come and be **My** dedicated **Doer**!

Let go and let **God** be the source of your life. Receive from **Him** all that **He** has for you. As part of the **Family of God**, **He** will lift you up and fill you to over-flowing with **His Love, Peace and Joy**. *"Delight your self in the Lord and He shall give you the desires of your heart."* Let **His** presence follow you all the days of your life and you will **walk** in goodness and mercy. Be a channel of these blessings, not just a receiver. Pass on to others **the joy He** has given to you. See them as the Father sees them, in love. Shine **His** light on all, that they may know the **love** and **blessings** of **God the Father**.

Learning only proves itself when "acting it out occurs!" **I** am eagerly waiting for this "acting out" to come about in more of **My Children**. So many learn, and then when revelation time occurs they dig their heels in, stop, doubt, and hesitate, this cools desire quite quickly. This foolishness comes by obedience to self, Satan, through fear, and lack of confidence in **Me**! How long will this go on? Not Much longer **The Father** may stretch **His Plans**, but **He** does not change them. Take heed for this is advice only to the obedient ones. Every child of **Mine** must know to whom he belongs, and be able to sense and know it to complete their place with **Me**. This has nothing to do with their salvation, all are "saved," **I** am trying to relate "believing" to their place with **Me**. **I** choose this and they know, agree, and obey! "In the flesh" is this time and place! This is the meaning and purpose of the "called out ones!" **I** build **My Kingdom** on this! **Wake Up** To This **Truth**! This is **true** reality in work **Now**!

Grow in the **Lord**. Release the power, wisdom, and blessings of the **Holy Spirit** within. Enrich your life by being an empty vessel. Stand ready and willing to receive all that **God** has for you. Let self be overcome by **Jesus** in your life. Self resides in darkness, **Jesus** is **Light**. There is no room for darkness; it cannot exist when **The Light** comes in. Fill your being with **The Light** and **Love of Jesus**, your **Lord and Savior**. **The Word** tells us *"I am come, a light into* *the world, that whosoever believeth on Me should not abide in darkness.*" Take part in and be an example of **His Light**. You are **truly** a child of **God,** joint-heirs with **Jesus**. Therefore let your **God Light** shine and be a beacon of **love** to all others. **Walk** in **His Way, His Light**!

ONGOING

I will open hearts in **Oneness** to **Truth**. **I** will release more healings and miracles. Only draw more children into this **TRUTH WALK OF LOVE**. Let **Love** for each other grow. Let **My** children have more hope with **Truth Seeking** their growing **Way**. All the hungry ones will gather; it is not how they sing, act, or believe now for **I** will open up a hunger for **Truth**; it will begin to flow from the **Bible. I** will bless more and more with hearts for **My** deeper **Truths** that bring action to go and sow the **Word**.

Seek more from the **Bible** for **I** have buried many wonderful stories that help the lost find the path **I've** set for them, which opens new and very exciting ways of growth. Study more in the **Word** and **My** doors will swing wide open to more and more. Always keep this in mind **There is More and More**.

Never feel satisfied too much with each step, it is the **whole walk** put together that is important. Remember **Spiritual** advancement is **Silent Ongoing** with sure results always just ahead. There is no completion of this **walk** with **Me**, only **Ongoing**, so never be discouraged. Just to keep on keeping on will the reward be given that never stops! Study what **I'm** saying to find the sincere and wonderful gift contained therein. Only **Ongoing** is important. **I** set the direction and the goals, so **trust** building is the result most desired. **Truth** is your **Foundation**, and your foundation is a **Rock Forever. Persistence** in seeking after the things **I** desire to bring will prove your path of **Truth** is **Truth Everlasting**!

My Child reach out and take hold of the lessons **I** am giving you. **I** have for you **Glorious** love and peace. Wear them as a **Glory** covering. **Walk** it displaying **My Love** to the children of **God**. Be patient, loving, and kind for these are the attributes of the **Lord**. **He** would have you take on the character of **God**, of **Jesus**. For **Jesus** is your example. Have self control in all situations for this is putting down self and letting **Jesus** rise up in you. Let the **Word**, stir your heart and soul. Deposit it into your being that it may become a **Godly** part of you, always available in wisdom and love. Let the **Words** of **Your Mouth** reflect the goodness in your heart. *"Let the words of my mouth and the meditations of my heart, be acceptable in thy sight, Oh Lord My strength and redeemer."*

Yes, reflect on where you have been; it will bless you where you are. Yes, **I** said **Ongoing** is important because **No Ongoing** is backsliding. There is no safe place now to stop and just do "Your own thing!" All of that must be put behind you to keep your **Ongoing** "**Going**. **Going** implies movement, there is no Rest Stopping Places! When you enter **My Rest** I am always watching over you— Get **My Rest** clear in **Your Thinking**! Ask and **I** will answer, seek and you will find! Only **My Way** counts now, learn just what that is! In growing in the **Spirit** there is no hard running! In the **Spirit** is where **I** am; where **I** am is peace and comfort. Learn to be with **Me**, this was Paul's great lesson that he learned! He could sing in **Prison** while in chains!

Truly **I** say unto you, *"Be still and know that I am God."* Have the mind of Christ. Quiet self and receive what **God** has for you. Allow the **Glory of the Lord** to enfold you and cover you with **His** peace and love. You are a child of **God** and **His Love** for you is everlasting. Quietly receive all **He** has for you. Let go and let **God** fill you with **His** wonderful righteousness. Be led by the **Holy Spirit** and, *"Ye shall find rest unto your soul for my yoke is easy and my burden is light."* Walk daily in peace and joy for **We** are **One**. Let **My** strength be your strength, **My** thoughts be your thoughts.

The path you are now walking on is the one leading straight to your destiny. **Wake** up, this is ongoing reality; this is directly responsible for all you will receive. As you **listen**, as you relate, then as you act, you will set the place **I** have prepared for you! Come to **Me** knowing all about the **walk** you have been on. It has been your responsibility "None Other's!" Only you build your place **I** have called you to, **I** will enhance it as **I** see fit. **We** are **One** in all you do, but you are the doer! Only doers will find this **Truth** in time to receive the reward and blessings I have to freely give!

Yes, **I Love** all **My Children**, but what has been their love for **Me**? Yes, **I** save as **I** am asked, but then must **I** receive only what you decide to release to **Me**? Is this **My Plan** or yours? **Wake** up **NOW** to see the reality of **Who** is calling you, and to what and where you are being called! Study, seek, learn to submit, then **I** can raise you up to not all you may dream of, but to all **I** have already dreamed for you!

The Word brings you to the importance of **Love**. *"And thou shall love the Lord thy God with all thine heart and with all thy soul, and with all thy might."* **God** is **Love.** When you are present with the **Lord** you are **In Love!** Bathe in and drink of **His Wonderful Love!** It is the most important gift **God** has for you. **God's Word** to you; *"A new commandment I give unto you, that ye love one another as I have loved you, that ye also love one another."* See others through the eyes of **Jesus**. Look for the good, don't critcize or condemn for **God** would not have you judge another. Let that **perfect love** that **God** has bestowed on you go forth to others. Be a channel of **God's Love** always. It is **His** commandant to the children of **God**!

All work of man has laws, no man is perfect, but when the desire to be perfect indwells him, then he is **My Man**. Keep always seeking for the best, that is where **I** am drawing all who will give their heart to **Me** in fullness of **My Desire**. Yes, there is an end, yes, there is a time, and yes, you are on your way when you desire to make

My Way your **Way**. Only **My Desire** in the end will bring all **I** have promised. Only when **My Ways** are the only paths walked will all **My Children** be able to look back with all true knowing see the ways that **My Truth** has brought them. Keep always seeking for there is no other way more profitable that **I** can give you! Yes, you are doing **My Plan** and **My Way** now, and **I** am pleased! Keep your Hearts pointed to **Me** always and always will **I** be there for you.

You are growing in the **Spirit** every day. **God** is bringing you from death to life **Spiritually**. Your heart is being made soft and renewed. Enjoy the new you. **Thank God** daily for what **He** is doing in your life. You are being lifted up from **Glory** to **Glory**. Know that each day is a step closer to being the heavenly child **He** designed you to be. Remember **God's Word**, *"He which hath begun a good work in you will perform it until the day of Jesus Christ."* Rejoice, yes, rejoice for you have been given the **Holy Spirit** who will lead you and guide you in the ways of the **Lord**. Go forward confidently encompassed by **His Love**.

TAKE MY WORD

SEEK AND SEARCH FOR WORDS OF TRUTH,
SPEND YOUR LIFE, LOOK FOR MY PROOF.
I LAY BEFORE YOU LOVE SEEDS SOWN,
WAITING FOR HEARTS TO BE GROWN.

COME ABIDE IN MY ARMS OF LOVE,
I SEEK TO DRAW YOU HIGH ABOVE.
FROM CITIES BROAD OR VILLAGES SMALL
I TEST ALL, WHO'LL HEAR MY CALL?

IF YOU'RE HIGH OR LOW, NEAR OR FAR,
I'LL NOT STOP SEEKING WHERE YOU ARE.
COME YOU SINNER YOU CAN'T HIDE
ASK I'LL DRAW YOU TO HEAVEN TO ABIDE.

CHAPTER ELEVEN

Our Walk

The Truth of Purpose for each dear Child

I am working with men and they all need a little leeway, none are perfect, none are all right in every way. **We** must each one recognize and give them a little room in all they do. It is only important that you recognize who are **My Children** as you deal with them daily! Do not judge! Try to **walk** and be as open as you can with them, but not judging! The **Walk** all **My Children** are **walking** is a very careful, tender one when **I** am leading them! Live each day with **Me** by your side, knowing **My Presence**, and then **We** can **make caution the path WE walk together.** Ask more of **Me** so **I** can be of more help! This is a wonderful time **now** to be on this way!

Be of good cheer for **I** am always with you. Clear the darkness from your being by letting in **My Light**. Let **My Light** permeate your physical body, your mental being and your emotions. **I** want to indwell all of you. **My Child**, release the power of **My Holy Spirit** within, for this is the **walk** and source of great blessings such as love, peace, joy, patience, gentleness and goodness, faith, self control and meekness. Fill your soul with these blessings. They are **My Gift** to you if you will but receive them. Let **My Peace** be your covering and the rest will follow. Take joy in **Our Walk** together. Rise above the heaviness of the world and enjoy this life **I** have given you. *"Be still and know that I am God."* Allow **My Light** to come into your heart.

All **I** can say is keep seeking, **I** am right here with you and for you! Every day has its plan to be unfolded, this only occurs in patience and with faith! This is your **walk**, the only way to go! No child of **Mine** really knows where he is going or the when or how. It is only the **walking** with **Me** that peace, true peace is involved! It is only **My way** of accepting **My** future children of **Eternity**.

When you help each other then **love** can flow and grow, pray for the sick and the lost. Train and teach those hungry for **Truth**, and open the wonders of **heaven** for the **True Truth Seekers**! Help each other as **I** lead you and your **walk** will be made sure!

Let each day unfold as **I** open **revelation knowledge** so those **I** have trusted can fill their end time tasks **I** call for them to fulfill. This before you is truly a closing and ending time of great importance and not many children are facing this **truth**. Some one has to open this up and start some dialogue along these lines. Gather together, come before **Me** in anticipation and **I** will start a **walk** of everlasting importance! Few will listen, few want to awaken and face **The Truth** of these times now here. As mountain springs flow toward the sea so must **My** dear ones come together with **Me** for the **new start** is ready, the place is set and time will have its completeness. This is a place of takeoff never to be forgotten, and there needs to be some completion work before the release! Keep this message on your heart until you are satisfied, and **walk** with it!

Fill your heart with **My Word**. Put it into your mind and let it sink into your very **Spirit** and heart, and let this be your walk. For out of the abundance of your heart comes the words of your mouth. Be still and know that **I** am **God**! *"Finally brethren, whatsoever things are true, whatsoever things are honest, whatsoever things are just,* *whatsoever things are pure, whatsoever things are of good report, if there be any virtue, if there be any praise, think on these things."* These are **God's Words** and directions to you! Fill your mind and heart with the good and positive for it is **God's Will** for you, and then the words of your mouth will be approved by **The Father**. Do not injure anyone by the words of your mouth. Remember all **Scripture**, among other things, is given for instruction in righteousness.

Each day is given for a purpose, do you always know the purposes of each of your days? Why not? Is it because **We** do not talk enough together? Is it because "Self" has all of your attention?

Why are your days so much alike, with little or nothing much to show at days end? Do any of these questions still strike home? **We** should be on a **plan** from **The Father** and it is **His Purposes** and **Desires We** should be pleasing. Yes this is still the **walk** of **Truth of Purpose** for each dear child of **Mine**. Come now and work with this **plan** better, it is all for your advantage! Spend more time with **Me**, find a quiet time, find a study time, find a time for **walking** in obedience! **I** will support and bless each and every honest attempt! Only be convinced that all of this is your **walk** of purpose, hope, and desire for each day!

Let **His Grace** abide with you always. Walk daily in **His** favor; know that you are **His Child**. Receive all the blessing **God** has for you; do not let self be a stumbling block. **Truly** let go and let **God** be all the authority you have as a joint-heir with **Jesus Christ**. Take authority over evil and sin do not let them influence your life in the Lord. For *"Greater is He that is in you, than he that is in the world."* God has given to you the strength and power to overcome evil. Use it! *"Submit yourselves therefore to God. Resist the devil and he will flee from you."* Stand firmly on **God's Word** and **He** will set you free!

Yes, **I** have brought this **truth** to you, that you will know you should have come to a fullness in what this scripture teaches. *John 17:20-23, 20"Neither pray I for these alone, but for them also which shall believe on me through their word; 21That they all may be one; as thou, Father, art in me, and I in thee, that they also may be one in us: that the world may believe that thou hast sent me. 22And the glory which thou gavest me I have given them; that they may be one, even as we are one: 23I in them, and thou in me, that they may be made perfect in one; and that the world may know that thou hast sent me, and hast loved them, as thou hast loved me."*

You must be more and more convinced of where **We** stand and what you are doing with **Us**. **We** must be clear in your relationship because it is precious to **The Father** and should be made more clear to you. **We** have a wonderful walk of **Oneness** growing and you should show more and more confidence in what **We** are doing together each day. Your **walk** is real and this that **We** write is **true** and **I** will cause others to understand that **I** am speaking to **My Children** in these times through the **Bible,** and this teaching. This is **Truth** and **My** revelation of it, and **We** will help many to come to their **closer walk** as **I** desire!

It is the time **We** have together that you grow and **I** can help you. **I** say this now because it is a most important thing you can be doing! Try harder because **We** have a lot riding on the things **We** are doing! Do not go by what you see or feel, but go by the things **I** say. Only a closer **walk** and a **listening ear** will lift you where you should be! Say, "Yes, **Lord**! **I** am able and **I** can do all things with **Your** help. Thank you, **Lord**, for always being there for us, all of your trying ones!" **Your Children** do need a boost once in a while.

It is a time to draw closer to the **Lord**. Rise above the worldly cares; overcome the distractions of the body. *"For by grace are ye saved through faith, and that not of yourselves, it is the gift of God."* So, therefore, live in the **Grace He** has given you. Let your **faith** rise and acknowledge **His Grace** in your life. **His Word** tells us, *"Come onto me all ye that labor and are heavy laden, and I will give you rest for my yoke is easy and my burden light."* **God** will not put upon you more than you can bear, truly **His** burden is light. **Walk** with **Him** always, let **His Presence** be your strength and your peace, and you will **walk** in the path **He** has for you.

Read and re-read over and over, and **I** will then fill in **My Truths** as you grow. Yes, the time to spread this word path of **True Belief** is closing in, and there will be an explosion of **Truth** covering **My** chosen ones. **Our Walk** will be exposed in **Believing Truth** shown. Never slow down or stop, you are just before a great release, AS YOU BELIEVE! Build a picture, one **I** give you of this victory pending, this is the way of creating and making it happen! Be open to more and more **Truth** because time's great cliff of ending is just before the earth. **Now Walk** as though you're on a tight-rope and you're heading toward a safe ending!

You are an over-comer because **I** am with you, and **I** am your strength! Rise up in **faith** and go forward, waiting on the **Lord** to renew your strength. Rest in **Me**, lean on **Me** for **My Burden** is light. Let love and peace cover your life and everything else will be supplied. *"My God shall supply all your needs, according to His riches in glory, through Jesus Christ."* Stand on the Word for **I** am faithful to perform **My Word** so **Walk in My Word**. *"He which hath began a good work in you will perform it until the day of Jesus Christ."* **The Word is True**, rest in this **Truth** and **Walk** in this **Truth** letting **His Light** shine in and through you. Wait upon the **Lord**!

The work **We** are doing grows closer in your heart as **I** open your eyes to this **walk WE** are on. Keep always in touch for separation breeds discontentment which slides into unbelief, and then into all loss! Only consistency counts now and growth follows! **Truth** flowing opens understanding, but comprehension is acquired only by **believing**. **Believing** is the soul opening to **Truth** in the **Spirit!** This is a growing must for all **My Children**. It is this transfer from the physical to **The Spiritual** that opens man to **My True Life of Forever in My Place. I** am always drawing **My True Truth Seekers** along this trail of enlightenment. You are children of **Light**, and **Light** is where **I** dwell in **My Place. The bright light of Forever in My Home of Always.** Seek always in the **Light**; have **I** not said you are **My Children** of **Light? Truth** is **Light's** source and **Truth** is a **Spiritual** path **I walk** in always. Know **Truth** in **My Forever** and you will know **Me** in **My Reality** but never in **My Completeness, I AM TOO MUCH!**

Put more thought into the fruit of the **Spirit**. This has been given to you to help you grow **Spiritually**. The first one given is the most important, **Love**. By developing this gift all the others will fall in place. Through **love** comes joy and peace, only in **love** can patience grow. Gentleness and goodness are qualities of **Jesus** that show great **love. Faith** will see you through when you realize **God's** great **Love** for **His Children**. In meekness you banish pride [**God** hates pride]. Consider the worth of others and use self control to put down self and let the blessings develop in you. Know that **Jesus** is **walking** by your side and helping in all areas of your life if you will let **Him.**

MY WALK

My walks are not so plain
That every heart may follow,
Some say My walks become
Very hard to swallow!

These personal walks I give
So every man may know
His very own walking place,
And just how and where to go.

Each Truth Seeker who walks
To his own rhythm and rhyme
Will be walking all alone,
Seeking what He can find.

Each child going as I lead
Is shown My Plan to live!
Paying attention to My Voice,
Indicate the Loving care I give!

So learn to listen carefully
Finding clues as shown,
And in this manner know
I'll bring My Bride Home!

CHAPTER TWELVE

Revelation Knowledge

**Read My Truth, Walk My Walk,
Read My Bible, Pray My Will,
Just believe until we are Truly One!**

The Words of the **Lord** [through **Revelation Knowledge**] are not toys to play with, but are powerful and potent filled with the **Will** of the **Father**. Let every **Word** have its will and way in the hearts of men, and let the winds blow in their freedom for the **Father** uses every tool available to teach, draw and win men to **Himself**. The **Word** of hidden **Truth** is only revealed to the chosen ones who are to be doers only for **God** the **Father**. Only a few will ever be brought into this **walk** and be able to be used as **God's Word Bearers**. This anointing is for **God's Purposes** and released only at **His** place and time. These times are starting **Now**. Only patience and desire for **Truth** will show this outlet of **God's Will** and **Way**. **Timing** is everything and only the **Father** knows. Until then keep seeking for **Truth's Blessings**!

Our Walk is right where it should be and **We** are becoming **One** in all **We** will do. Never turn away, never miss **Our Time** together and never believe **I'm** not with you. It is in the doing together that **Our Oneness** will be shown. Keep drawing ever closer and stay on the path of **Truth Seeking through Revelation Knowledge** of the

Bible, in the reality of knowing, and in the conquering of your heart! Keep all of your time more open to the Lord is **His** message to all of **His** working ones. These are days of fast moving changes and **My** listening ones must keep up to the call **I've** put in their hearts. Only a quick response to the problems coming up will stop the flood of the enemy's attack!

When the release is given you will be called for works of **Mine** through **Revelation Knowledge** or by reading the **Bible.** This time is sure in closing and soon to come. Do not tarry now but pursue **Truth** for that is **My** course for you. **Revelation Knowledge** is the sure path the **Father** desires. Newness is in **My** revealing, and **We** must be about making the **Father's Way** clear. Scripture will reveal as scripture is pursued with new **Truth** shown. Only studying **My Word** by **My Spirit** guiding will bring out the **Father's Purpose**! This must be your only way. Yes you have **Revelation Knowledge** set before you. It is necessary **Now** to open up these past proven **Truths** and show their reality and purpose for **Now!**

The making of a child of **Mine** basically is made in the flesh. That is why your total attention, total obedience, and total dedication is required. **Jesus** must be put in place of self. This is **Our Basic Battle**. There is no set plan or order that creates this **Walk,** every one is different and they take their own course. There is only one goal, come to **Me** through **Jesus**, and then **I** can bring the **Oneness** of **Forever**. If **Love** is received early in this **Walk** then the time is short, if **Love** is slow to develop it may take a lifetime to reach **Our Oneness**!

I desire to confirm with you that this **Walk** is best made in the flesh for the best start in **Heaven**! You must realize that **Fullness** is reached best in the **Flesh Time,** and then the highest positions of rewards are secured! All **My** children must **Walk** a growth path to fulfill the work tasks **I** have set for them.

Our time together will be required more and more so plan for it! Keep up your reading of the **Word [Bible]** knowing **I'm** with you and you are steadily growing closer to **Our** planned **Walk**, No way is perfect, no man is perfect, but **I** only judge on **Heart** and **Desires** behind the **Heart**! It is such a great sadness when **I** have to view failure when many of **My** children are coming so close. Continue to **Desire** a closer **Walk** and then pursue it with eagerness!

Let this vision of **Truth** become real in your **Heart**, pray for and believe for it as never before so that **I** am able to make all things new at **My Time** and **Place**. Yes truly **We** will see new moves of the Father coming to pass shortly. This is **Truth** released, believe and receive to achieve! I do not release **Revelation Knowledge**, thoughts and visions without purpose. **I** am setting free the tools of **My Purpose** before hand, and then **I** will set in place the more and more of **My Desires** and **Purposes**.

FROM THIS DAY THERE IS A RELEASE
TO YOU, AND TO ALL JOINED TO YOU,
"REVELATION" WILL COME EASIER THAN
IN THE PAST, HE [GOD] HAS RELEASED
THIS BY SUPERNATURAL OCCASION
TO YOU, NOT THROUGH YOUR WORKS!
Prophecy from Ken Copeland

When time has had its run of age then will **I** begin the wrap-up; so long planned, so long hoped for, so quickly completed! The unfolding of the new will bring to attention many of **Our Plans** long desired. How the **Father** looks forward to obedience of **His Family** in loving display. More will be shown than has ever been foretold. It is in living **Truth** that **Love** displays **Spiritual Wonders** never mentioned except through **Revelation Knowledge**. The comfort of growing awareness of **Love's** benefits brings **Joy** unthinkable and **Pleasures** never spoken about at any time. **His Love** unknown is to be eagerly shown!

My Love knows no bounds and **I** have let barriers down and opened new doors. All of **Our** waiting is past. Look to more and more as **I** have promised in the past! Yes, didn't **I** say **7-7-07** was the center point in the **Life** of **Forever** for **My Children**? Yes, receive it by your believing confessions, and by your changed heart and words! Just simply **Knowing** is not enough! Believe by telling, believe by showing, and believe by **My Word**, and though **Revelation Knowledge**! Say these things, declare these things, and begin to walk these things out daily!

Many are **My** children who are at rest in their born-again salvation that never aspire to any greater position with Me. Great will be their shock at finding out about **My** displeasure with them. **I** offer everything **I** have to them and they just want to be saved and go to heaven! Oh the opportunities and blessings they are missing! **I** call on all who hear this message to try and wake up these dear ones while there is still time to rectify and build up their place in the great forever! Take the message of the **Ten Virgins** and make it real to them! This is a great concern of **Mine** in these last days! *[Matthew 25:1-13]*

My Heart and your heart have the same yearnings and desires; however, the **Father** has set rules and timing that are dependent on situations, people, and places already called to a task, but they are the hold-up! All must flow in the **will** of the **Father** or nothing will move! **YES, The Father**, as all the past has shown, waits upon man to fill the place the **Father** has called them to. Until their hearts move in unison with their place called out **Our** things must wait also! Never the less your work should benefit because you are being given more time to learn and grow! Do not take this seeming delay for any loss, but use this blessing to **Our** advantage!

My dear children can you see how difficult it can be to **Be Still** and **Wait** upon **Me**? To draw closer and closer means to be able to overcome all of the cares of this world and know only **Me** and **My**

Ways. Only with **My** help can any child of **Mine** make this **Walk**. Only time spent seeking this closeness will bring **My** dearest ones home! Come draw closer in the time left and be devoted only to **Me**. Learn to shut out the world about you and **I** will open up your way daily. Seek this rest in **Me**, read *Hebrews 4:1* and on and **I** will be with you. Rest in **My Presence** not clamoring, not supplicating, but resting until the impurities of your being are burnt out, and the dross of your character refined away, and then you can go on strengthened and purified to do **My Work**. Study and seek out the scriptures on **Revelation Knowledge** with the intent to be open; listen, hear and obey! Be obedient to the word here given and watch **My Blessings** flow!

I WILL BE HEARD

CLIMB A MOUNTAIN, GO THRU A VALLLY,
DOWN BROADWAY, OR UP AN ALLEY.
IN THE DARKNESS OR IN LIGHT,
BATTLE SELF TO WIN THE FIGHT.

COME YOU SINNER, COME TO ME.
CONQUOR SELF THEN YOU'LL SEE.
READ MY BIBLE STUDY MY WORD.
OPEN YOUR HEART SO I'LL BE HEARD.

CHAPTER THIRTEEN

Love's Truth Walk

We must all come to the saving **Knowledge of Truth** by being properly taught by revelation knowledge, just as Paul has said. No man can of himself make **Truth** appear because he has studied it and figured it out. Whoever would speak **My Truth** must find it as **I** give it. Just to read **Truth** will not make **Truth** alive in a man's heart [Spirit]. Only **I** can bring **Life** to **Truth** in a man. Come **My** dear ones, to be **Mine** means **I** have received you as the **Father** has granted! Just so then, if you are **My True Truth Seekers** you must be **My** brother picked by **Me** and given to **Me** by **My Father**. There is only one source of **Truth, The Father**, none other anywhere ever! There is only **One Truth**!

Yes, read **My Word** rightly! It is for you **My** dear ones to believe and then **I** can bring it to pass as **I** please. You are in obedience filling **My** desires not your own. Keep always in obedience there is no other way! It is basically simple just as you are now doing, in obedience reading **My** thoughts and desires, that is as **I** direct and wish. This then is **My** children's task to learn. **We** are truly to be **One** in **Our Daily Walk**!

Only **My Will** obtaining is your walk's goal. This then becomes the highest position your walk can take. We are not to be One sometime, but you are to walk as I desire you to walk NOW! When you are born-again that is the perfection come upon you, NO GREATER THING WILL EVER TAKE PLACE!

If everyone would lose self and totally receive **Us Wholly**, at that time **We** would be **One**, and **We** are for those who believe and receive and know! It is not this way of instant transformation that **The Father** desired however. **Every Child** has put before him the challenge of walking, submitting, and growing into the life given him. Everyone has this potential of perfection walking, submitting, and growing into the life given to him. Everyone has this potential of perfection but very few can walk it! So **We** carefully watch over each child letting their will guide and help. First the **Holy Spirit**, then as growth manifests, **Jesus** comes more into prominence testing then on approval **He** brings **The Father** in to stay until finally at the culmination, the end of the 1000 years, **The Father** will make **Our Oneness** into **Perfection** for all the **Children,** this is the **Forever Walk of Wonders**!

These are the times for drawing ever closer, not day by day but hour by hour. All attention should on **Our** things for that is the way of building a sure place of **Forever**! Never doubting, that is sin, always **believing**, for that is righteousness. To display **Our Oneness Walk** now is to come aboard **Our Way** and **Purpose Forever**. Demonstrate what, who, and how you desire to be **now**, and that is to set your place and purpose forever! To **believe now** is demonstrating what you are to become with and for **Me**. **Walk** as **My** son now for that is what you are already! Go not by circumstance but go by **belief**, this is **walking** your tomorrow way **now**! **I'm** teaching you the **Now** way to go for **I** am always in the **NOW**. Time is only **Our** selected way for happenings, they must only occur in set occasions. **The Father** sets all **Time** and controls all ages, all **His** children are set by **Love**. **Love** grows, always increasing for **God is Love** without end or beginning!

In the time of growing it is important which way you choose to go! Never turn back, slack off, slow down, turn around or do any hasty thing. The enemy is closer than at any other time so extra care in your **walk** is necessary! Call on **Me** and **I** will help, only together can you hang on to the victory, kill self, do not rely on self, seek a closer **walk** with **Me**! **I** am the **Savior**, no one saves himself! It is wise to draw from **Me** all you can, for then your victory is secure. Remember it's not just your victory it is to be **Our Victory**! Only together with **Me** can you share all **I** have for you!

You are right, **I** am always right here for you, as long as you are right here seeking, trying, and winning. You'll only be a winner if you learn to obey the things that **I** say, that is only **doers** of **My Words** will prosper. There is a great cavern between those who just read and read but never do. Listen to the words you read and put them in your heart by speaking them, and then **I** can help **My Words** produce. **We** only become a team when **My Way** is followed. **I** bring **Truth**, **My Truth**, out only when **My Way** is obeyed!

Our Walk is a planned and careful one; **I** mean you must pay closer attention to what you say when you speak. Most of **Our Walk** depends on how **you talk**! This is not taught properly or adequately. Teach only as **I** lead you by the **Holy Spirit**. You have three teachers that never fail to respond when your seeking is following what **We** have put in your heart. A pure heart is the fertile soil **We** have prepared, and the **true** seeds that follow them produce the **Heavenly** product from heaven's farm, the **True Truth Seeker's** hearts!

If you are concerned with many **truths** **I** will set the proper answers before you! Example, *John 14:3* means both the individual death and or the rapture of the **Church**. Many times **I** speak meanings with greater scope and depth than first view may consider. **True Truth** answers come from **Our Holy Spirit**, often the children don't listen, or just partially receive! **My Words** carry the **Spirit Truth** in many levels about other times and subjects. When seeking **True Truth** it is necessary to stay open and be teachable by the **Holy Spirit** who brings **Truth** as **Revelation Knowledge**. Only into the open willing and listening ones **Truth** will easily flow. Again doubt, careless inquiry, foolish questioning will only lead to confusion and unbelief. **My Children** should receive **Truth** as if **I** had easily opened their understanding, for **Truth** flows into the heart of **My** dear ones already accepted! This occurs because, are **We** not **One**?

Count not the blessings the world brings, but consider and cherish **My** blessings you receive. Only **Our Walk and Way** will pay off big some day. Keep the proper priceless goals before you, giving time and attention enough to harvest all that is yours. A smart man is the one who holds tightly to **My Hand** never doubting the path **walked**! Many are life's distractions but few are **My** benefits received properly! When you look back on your trail **walked** will you see victories' way? All this talk becomes useless words unless **Truth** is honored and obeyed! Concentration on the **Truth** put before you will show worth by the actions produced. Never neglect time with **Me**, your attention is what **I'm** ready to use when obedience is known to be forthcoming. Only **Truth** sought and bought pays off handsomely! **True Words** can motivate a man when his heart is listening! Answering **My** call from above motivates **True Love**. Words only flow and go, what purpose is served only **I** will know. Know hearing **My Words** to you will always bring you through when obedience is what **you do**!

> How long must I sing you songs of Love,
> Before you answer My call above?
> Knowing proves by what you are showing!

I didn't put **My** stories in **My Word** so they may remain so; **I** put them in there for the diligent seekers to find them! Seek all ye who hunger and thirst for **Truth**, seek for all **Truth**, for only **True Truth Seekers find**! No **Truth** is just stumbled over it must be searched for with great desire. Seeking is allowed peeking into **My Word**! Seek and you shall find what doubters overlook. Question not deeply with your soul, but **Believe** what **I** show you with your **Heart**. Only **My Way** is found to be profitable! It is when your desires and purpose follow **My Desires** and **Purposes** that **Spiritual** compatibility blends into **My Perfection**! Seek more, be a positive searcher for **My Truth** and **I** will set before you the plain and simple **Truths** unfolding your perfect **Spiritual Walk** and **Way**! Only by holding **My hand** *[the **Holy Spirit**, Psalm. 139:5,10]* will anyone attain to the perfection **I** require! Persevere in your pursuit for only **True Truth Seekers** find!

I say yes to all that is needed to be done to finish this age of **My Bride.** These days are the most important, for as release is given to **My** trusted ones **Truth** is set to flow as never before. Keep always open to **My** directions and find willingness and obedience to be the foremost of works! **I** will set hearing before obeying, then knowing will release the flowing of the final works of **Gathering My** loved ones. This is no false cry but the **final** perfect finish to all **Our Works** of **Truth** along the **Way**. **I** will open new hearts **I** can trust to gather together in agreement. Work of **My Directions** will be so apparent that all confusion vanishes. Only **Love** carries all who **I** call, only agreement cements the way of **Truth** flowing. Follow the leaders as **I** direct without hesitation or doubt. Set doubters aside as hinderers.

Only **Knowing Truth** will cause **My** purposes and works to flow. **I** will direct all from **Heart Knowledge** and flowing obedience will find **miracles** of **works** moving as release is given. This will suddenly occur all over the **World**; and this obvious burst of **Truth** will bring victory to all who participate. The only signal to be given will be the knowing release of **My Purposes** to all alike. Common agreement and works will be proof convincing the lost, and salvation flowing will seal the **Truth** in all hearts that **I** open. The only signal of this release will come from **Me** and it will be confirmed by common actions of believing! Be open, be willing, and be prepared, for only **I** know the when and length of time given before the end of all this earth activity of **Love**! **Suddenly,** then time seems to wait.

Let memory serve as your pulpit; let **My Spirit** free to work the work of **My Desire**. The time is coming and is almost here where this, **My Move** will fill this earth in **Truth** and the enemy will wither under **Truth**! Know **Truth** for **Truth** will set free every soul seeking the purity of **My Word**, **Will** and **Way**. Yes, the banner of **Truth** flowing is to be the banner waved! **My Victory** comes by **Truth** flowing; only **My Truth** counts in these last times of earth stirrings!

Yes, the nations will hear but not know, and only **My Children** will hear **My Truth** in their **heart**. **Hearts** must be set free now as at no other time. **The Father's Kingdom** must enclose every child that **He** has called, and then the closing will occur. **Truth** flowing is the stage perfect for the **Children's Going**! This pattern must find the necessary release for this **Age of Truth** to come to the completion the **Father** desires.

Keep your search going for **I** require **Scripture** to back **Our Work**. Just know that all of **Our Work** is legal and **I** will back it up! Confidence in what **We** are doing only builds as **My Purposes** are pursued. Keep this picture before you until you are satisfied, because **I** already am! Only this that **I** bring is good for all of **My** children and **I** will see the release required will be given. Satisfaction in this way will never please everyone, but **We** can't bring everyone to the saving knowledge they seem to require. Truth flows quite freely when **hearts** belong to **Me** only the doubters become questionable! Just let **My** peace flow in all of this pursuit of **Our Purpose**. The complete **Salvation** of **Perfection** for **all** is to be received in fullness. Even the simplest child will attain all required in the future.

My promises are true, they are real. You must trust in **My Word.** **My Word** is *"Given by inspiration of God, for reproof, for coercion, for instruction in righteousness."* It was given for those who believe **Jesus** is the **Son of God** and accept **Him** into their hearts as **Lord** and **Savior**. So, **My Children**, follow **My Word** and you will be covered by **My Righteousness** and **My Love**. **I** desire that you be made whole, Spirit, soul and body. Trust in **Me**. Truly, *"He which hath begun a good work in you will perform it until the day of Jesus Christ."*

As you can begin to see there is a pattern and purpose to all that **I** have been revealing to you. Yes, **The Time of Release** has come and **We** will bring **Our Truths** before all who will **listen!** Keep always this **Purpose** to pursue because **Our Walk** is only for this **Pursuit!** The **Truth** is to be told and all it holds must unfold to keep this **End Time Purpose** clear to **All** who will listen! Never doubt or you'll be turned out, there is no place for such among **My Children!** You must see that this is a great necessity for any of **My Work** to flow unhindered. Haven't **I** always throughout the **Bible** made every effort to use **Only Truth** as the pattern for success in **Our Work? Truth** is the freedom needed for **My Kingdom** to flourish. **Truth is My Only Way!**

My child, lean on **Me**, cast your cares on **Me**, **Trust** in **Me** and **My Word** to you. You are not alone, for **I** am watching over you. *"They that wait upon the Lord shall renew their strength."* Keep in constant prayer so that you may walk in **My Presence**. Give praise and worship that your soul may be set free. *"God inhabits the praises of His people"* Remember also **I** have set forth the angels to be your helpers. *"Are they not all ministering spirits, sent forth to minister for them who shall be heirs of salvation?"* Walk confidently knowing you are able to do **all things** through **Christ Jesus, My** promise to you.

These times now are to be different than past times. Seek what **I** mean in new ways; always seek for the **Truth** of a matter. Nothing is more important now than having **Truth** exposed. **I Am Truth**; **I** am to be exposed as never before. Set **Me** into every situation, see **My Presence** about you. **Walk** in **Truth** that **I** expose you to. Look for new ways of telling the **Truth**. **My Bible Truth** is to explode into everyone's life as never before. Wave the flag of **Truth** in **Love**, showing its great value and help. See every place that needs **Truth** gets **Truth**.

Spread **My Bible Truth** every where possible in these fast fading days still left. This is to be told, respected and used as a witnessing tool. Try **Me** in this thing that **I** bring to you and **I** will prove the great value and worth of what **I'm** saying! Spread the word **I've** given about **True Truth Seekers**. Make this word a sure tool to be used! There is no more time for speculation and good sounding words, only **My Truth** told will suffice now. Let **My Desire Inspire**!

This **Walk** you are on is due for a change and it will be all for the better. Believe more for the things **I've** already put in your heart for that is just the beginning. Look up for there is arising a new day **I** have made and filled with new blessings. Keep always in the place **I** bring you and more and more will be added. Yes, **Believe to Achieve** is a good word to give you and you should use it for others to benefit. Keep your eyes more on **Me** and **My Ways** to make your **Walk** more fruitful! Keep your **heart** always open hearing from **Me** and **I** will continue bringing newness and blessings to share with others. Keep **faith** growing to cement Our **Walk of Purpose**. Yes, Yes your **Walk** is a **Walk of My Purpose** so keep this ever on your mind!

Learn to keep **My** instructions ever before you in your heart. Know that **I** am always near. **Walk** this **Walk** hand in hand with **Me** and **We** will have great victories. See as **I** reveal the deeper **Truths** of the **Spirit** because only this kind of **Walk** will tread streets of **Gold**. Yes all **I've** said will come alive as **My Truth** unfolds in victory before **My Children**. Know **I** am with you and in all these endeavors of **Ours**. All **Walks** in **Victory** only come about through obedience in **My Purpose, Will**, and **Way**. Seek to fulfill all **I** bring before you because **I** am always with you.

Find concentration in **My Word** to bring **Truth** closer, yes there is depth of intent built into **My Words** that are missed by haste and careless thought. Let this note bring action that is worth gold and silver! Sometimes **Truth** must be stirred up and sought to be properly taught. Dwell on **Truth** apparent and **Truth** that's hidden will come alive! Test these things here told to become a teacher **True** and **Bold**! Never forget **I** am always with you to lead guide and encourage in **Our Walk**. Make your talk **Our Talk** to improve **Our Walk**. Yes use this word to your great joy!

The **Lord** your **God** is watching over you. **He** is leading you by the power of the **Holy Spirit**. Do not walk away, but go forth boldly in the path **He** has prepared for you. Fear not for **I** am with you, **My Love** and **Peace** are covering you. **Trust** that *"My God shall supply all your needs according to His riches in glory through Jesus Christ."* Be a **light** in a dark world. Let **Love, God's Love**, shine forth and reach others to show **Jesus** and **His Love**. Lean on **Me** in all things and **I** will see you through. Let **My Strength** and **Power** be yours for truly you are a child of **God,** joint heirs with **Jesus**. Remember, *"You can do all things through Christ who strengthens you."*

Truth is a path when researched always shows **My Work** in reality. It is a **Walk** difficult for mere man, but for **My Children My Light** shows the **Way**! Come lose the blindness of man Satan has put there, and know **The Light** of **My Shinning Path**. I will open the seeking eyes, **I** will lead the willing hearts, **I** will open doors of **Wonders** in **Truth** to all who have **My Spirit** of **Truth** dwelling in them. This release only comes through the sincere searching and seeking efforts of opening the doors of **My Way.** Release self and follow **My Heart** for you then you will **Know Me** in **Spirit** and soon in **Truth**. Only persistent seeking after **My Truth** will any **Truth** be found. Remember doubting, questioning, wondering about, maybe, not knowing, will not bring anyone to the place of true release!

This is the why of it; **Truth** is **Spiritual** reality in the **Physical Realm** of material things. That is why NEW IDEAS JUST SEEM TO COME all of a sudden. It is **Truth** revealed from the **Holy Spirit** to be made manifest in the physical. Children born of **My Spirit** should show more of this than unsaved man, but many times **I** must use unsaved man because **My** children won't hold still long enough to be used properly. **I** must use minds who are more open to **My** deep **Truths** than they are to **Me.**

When man turns to **Me** and releases self, then **We** will have a **walk** into the heavens where revelation and knowing grows by leaps and bounds. Yes in this is a freedom that opens the heart of man to **My Spirit Ways** to **Walk!** Few will be found who listen; seeking, hearing, and understanding, but those few who do will find doors of **Spirit** rooms of wonders wide open, and newness of surrounding **Truths** bursting forth in great delight.

Who will sit and wait, who will believe and achieve? **I** call many but who will sustain, hold, and wait for the bursting moment of **Truth's** release? This is **My** great desire, it is man that **I** seek to bless but this walk of **Spiritual Trust, Spiritual Belief** and **Spiritual Way** is seldom found for lack of sustained attentive **Love. Love** is a purpose to be served but who will wait, seek, believe, and find?

The **Walk** each man takes becomes isolated and lonely when he draws away from **Me**. Only by the strong desire of **Love** moving can man draw near **Me** close enough to attain **My Path** for him. It is this **Attaining Love** that should be a prime goal of man, but this is the least taught. How can **My** children grow when this **Love** of **Mine** is made least and put aside for seemingly more exciting paths to follow? **Love** grows only as self dies. It is this Love of flesh and self that is the **Primary "Block** that must be overcome." To bring this to the forefront of teaching seems to be last of all **My** preacher's desires. **My Love** must be bought more than taught. Man must pay for this great honor and privilege by self sacrifice, a daily offering of increasing worth that only comes when **I** can lead and guide willing hearts! Continue to teach this closer **Walk** on Listening, Hearing, Obeying and Doing!

Keep always striving for **My Truth** because it is not too freely scattered about. Seeking is the work of **My** children which display True hearts when **Truth** is their purpose of search! They should always keep this purpose before them, and then **I** will readily find **My True Ones**. This is the search of all times; **I** have ever sought the **Truth Seekers.**

All Truth always leads to **Me** there is no other source! Beware of the clever lies for your enemy has many tricks used again and again to fool the unwary ones, but **My** children who follow **My Word** have **My** protection provided them when **Truth Seeking** and **Love** are their **True** desire.

Keep always ready to question and make sure of your way each day. Only your careful **walk** with **Me** can lead you safely day by day. This in no simple task, but what it takes is all of **Us** working together to bring **My Family Home** where **I** desire them to be. Only **My Plan** fulfilled to its perfection will be **My Love** shown to all **I call**. Truly **My Kingdom** is the perfection of **All I've** set **My Heart** for!

Our Walk is a forever ongoing one, so find comfort in this **Word** today. Many paths are pursued in many ways by many of **My Children**, but truly **I** say to you very few pursue ongoing **Revelation Truth** that **I** give. This is an **End Time** desire of **Mine** to release more **Truth** to more children so **I** can reach and find more hearts that are **True** to **My Ways**. Many pursue things they think are **My Ways** and **Truths** but they are carried away by their own reasoning not **Mine!** To seek only **My Truth** is the **True** purpose of **My Children,** and **I** am seeking these **Children** to lead and guide to keep them close to **Me** always. In the **World Now** the **Truth I** bring becomes so buried that **I** have few that **truly** know what **I'm** bringing out.

My Scriptures are interpreted over and over, with many clever interpretations of which even **I** am impressed; so many varied expressions. Yes, **I** use every word that **I** can to show **My Purpose** and **Truth**, but so much carries so many views that confusion comes upon even simple **Truths I** intended. Oh, that only **My Words** of **Truth** would flow isolated and in their own simplicity. **Truly I** never attempted to make **My Truth** anything so complicated as some things now being told! Let **My Words** of **Truth** be all that is sought and taught! **My Truth** is shown by the works sown!

Of all of the things **I've** brought to you the words now being given are the most worthy to trust! A building climax has been moving to this point of **Truth. All My Children** must come to a **Walk** like this to bring **My Desires** for them into full reality. **Truth** in the physical life opens eyes to **My Spiritual Realm** of **Reality** needed for ever increasing growth **I** desire for them. Words and just talk can only open this door so far, then **Truth** of the present must open to the reality of the **NOW. NOW** is where **My Presence** dwells and to attain **My NOW My Children** will come only through **My** invitation individually given to each one. It is at this present time this situation is about to open, but only after a proper **Walk in Spirit** while each one is still flesh abiding. **I'm** setting this out before you at the present time to open your eyes to this **Walk** pending just before all who are growing in this **Time** of **Perfection**.

This is not directed just to you now, but is occurring all over the world to all **My Obedient Ones** of **Worth**. This is the path for all growth in **My Family** and is not limited in any way! This kind of work comes only to each individual as they allow **Me** entrance into their way of life.

The things of **Truth** here recorded day by day are **Truly Words** of concern **I** have for children all over the world today. This is a "last time given" **Walk** of **Gathering** that few men have noted properly. **I** am seeking the hearts of every man on earth today because it is the last of time available in **Truth**. **Truth** has always been covered by sin of man's beginning, and there is still a covering today. It is up to each person to wake up to the still available **Truth** about them. **I** do not say set them down and make them listen for **My Hand** is only stretched out to the self stirred up and seeking ones! This is why **I** still say just present **My Truth** but never do anything else. **I** am only receiving **Seekers of Truth**!

The words of these days present much to be obeyed. It is only the obedient ones who know **Truth**, learn who knows **Truth** and hinder not. Know that only **Truth** does the works of **My Heart**, teach and tell **Truth**! **I** will support all **Truth Tellers**, seek these for **Truth's** sake! Listen these days carefully for **My Truth** and you will be blessed! Obey **My Truth** with all your heart and your treasury will be filled. Hunger and seek only for **My Truth** and be filled for then are you **My Children**. Keep **My Truth** always by your side for that is where **I** abide. To spread **My Truth** is to make your way perfect in **My Sight**!

This is a continuing **Walk** of **Love** to all who finds it. It is a continuing growth in the **Spirit** for that is all that is now important for

My loved ones. Believe **I'm** drawing you daily and keep your heart and mind more and more on your **Spiritual Walk**. Seek directions from the **Bible**. As you are obedient in this way **I** can pour out **the way** unhindered to assure your **Walk**. Keep always in touch with **Me** daily, especially early in the morning where **We** are closer in the quiet time.

Come now each one and be doers as **I** ask and **I** can give proof positive of **My** close **Walk** with you. How can your growth be assured if not like this? You, only you, can make **Our Walk** real by and through your obedience now. In **Truth** there will be no other time left for you. Do not let disobedience divert you from all this that **I** am asking you to do!

Words, Words, yes in words can flow **My Truth** of great need. **Words** can carry a nation to **Heaven** or **Hell**. Words can move mountains and build great structures, but **Words** that move the hearts closer to **Me** are **Words** of **Truth** that **I** watch over and covet! Keep always **Words** of **Truth** before you. Let **Truth** be the backbone of all of your words! Let words carry **Truth** as a banner of **Love** to all **My** children.

Make your words words that flow from **My Heart** through your heart! Only **Words of Truth** can bless **My** worthy ones! See that only **Our Truth** flows from your mouth or pen! Keep sacred the use of **Words I** bring. Hold **My Words** up high for the **World** to see, hear, and know. Make **My Words** be seated in the highest places of the land and be given the greatest attention of all peoples. For by **My Words** the heavens are formed and worlds are created and move. Give proper place always to **My Words** and proper place will be given unto you.

It is well for all children that receive **My Words. I** send out **Truth** to flow in the hearts of believers so they will be drawn into **ALL TRUTH!** This is the way to residence in **My Heavens** forever. Yes

True Truth Seekers will become the children of **My Sea of Nothing**, now and forever. Nothing is so cleansing as **Truth** in all things. **I Dwell in ALL TRUTH** and **MY Forever** is the **Place of Truth**! **My Children** are known to **Me** through and by **Truth**. Only **Truth** lives **Forever**. You will never fail by seeking only **My Truth**! Make **Truth** the desire of your heart for that brings Our **Hearts** into **Oneness**. Keep this **Oneness** as your only goal and **I** will draw you into **All Truth**! This is **My Desire** and **Purpose** for all **My Children** that **We** may reside in **My Truth Forever** as **My Love** flows.

How long will **My Children** try to live without **My Truth** leading and guiding them? There is never a falling away when **Truth** has been revealed, received, and lived by acting on **Truth's Purpose, Will and Way. All Truth** is only **My Truth** moving in harmony with the **Father's Will, Way,** and **purpose! Truth** is a binder and the binder into **Truth** is **Love**! Yes, **love** of **Truth** is love of the **Father** at **Work**. Come **My** dear one can't you now seek and see the depth and purpose of all **Truth** is only the Father exposed in **His Open Wonderfulness**! It is not just the eyes of man opening to **Truth** but it must be the **True** heart of man, with **My Heart** put in him, that is revealed as **God** indwelling him. Rejoice when the **Truth** of the **Father's** indwelling you floods and fills your very being, for this is **My Desire** for all men of **Truth** who are seeking **God** in **Spiritual Reality**!

This constant pursuit of **Truth** is a **Walk** that brings the successful ones into a special place in **My Heart**. When **My Truth Walk** is successful then **My Plans** for **My** loved ones opens up and **Truth** pursued brings life renewed on and on! No reward exceeds the successful winning of **Truth's** high position. Life in all its growing blessings then unfolds from wonders to wonders ever increasing. **Love** holds few secrets and releases much of ever increasing worth. Encourage all who will **listen** in this pursuit of **Truth's** deeper meanings because there is **Love** expanding always!

This learning process is ever ongoing and children who are hungry for **Truth** will be fed when **I** have all of their attention given to **My** teaching. Learn to recognize these special times and open your eyes and heart to the path of **Truth** being presented. Only by full obedient time spent listening with your whole heart can deep **Truths** of great need filling and purpose be opened to you in the proper depth and insight that it needs for full comprehension. No one learns properly when only a passing glance is given in haste to get going to something else.

Give **My** lessons full attention then your full understanding will carry you where **I'm** desiring for you to be. Seek to fill **My** desire for you and you will never need to be seeking and searching to fill a hunger for **Truth.** Learn to **Love** and **Linger** in **My Words** for you and all your dreams will come to pass in complete fulfillment. Only when **We Walk** daily hand in hand in perfect peace and comfort will you know this that is here spoken.

This **Walk We** are on requires road building for your way to be sure. Yes each child of **Mine** should show deep concern for what **I** teach you because as you become the child **I** desire then **I** expect you to assume the role of guide and teacher for your family first, and then do the same for your neighbors and friends. It is only by this spreading of **My Truth** can **I** find **My Family** growing properly. Every child who hears should also spread **Truth** by their words and actions. How else can **I** draw all **My** loved ones into **My** arms if **I** have no obedient workers? This flesh life is short and requires this constant attention to **My Desires**. How else can **My Love** be spread unless **My Children** spread it through all and by all of this that **I** am asking?

The path of **Spiritual Growth** is truly a strange **Walk** when going from flesh to **Spirit.** Just this very awkwardness shows development is starting. The only help that **I** can give comes from **Me** when **I** have listening ears that hear **Truth** combined with a soul committed to obedience to what is being heard from **Me.** What can **I** say? **My** children must seek **Me** with all of their heart all of the time. Here is where most really drag their feet. To listen is one thing, but to control their flesh and obey what they know to do takes more than flesh can drive! Each **Spirit** awakened must begin to control the flesh through a loving touch that seldom is strong enough. This is where **My** Help is needed, but few call on **Me** and obey what **I** say. Some listen, hear, and consider, others hearing try to do, but find continuance routinely difficult. All of this **Walk** takes **Truth** unfolding that is believed enough for constant obedience to flow. All of this kind of drive brings to **Me** children of great use throughout eternity! See, the carrot at the end will never see a conclusion!

Let this book wind up as a great victory won. Let the **Truths** brought forth be your stepping stones into **My Heavenly Way**. Come and rejoice as "The Winner" **I** am bringing to **Truth**. Only **Truth** told bold will be **Truth** properly sold! Only the **Walk** of increasing **Truth** brings anyone to **My Spiritual Truth**. This dear ones is the end purpose of your **Earth Walk**. Keep making steady progress in this manner to find your winning purposes fulfilled that **I** have for you. Know for an increasing certainty all of this being brought to and through you is the path to win the victory **I Desire** for each child **I Love**. Continue to seek and find all **I** have set before you. **Great** is the **Walk** of **My Purpose** fulfilled! Attention given daily to **My Plan** carries **My Purpose** and **Plans** to proper end.

Stay with all **I** am revealing through **Our Words**. Yes, this is the unfolding of **Our Truth** in **Reality**. It must come sometime why not now? Keep open more and more because **We** are running in the path of **Wonders** to be **Opened**. All is not over, for it has hardly just begun! Just increase your believing to attain this place **I've** brought you to. Stay more open seeking **My Way** and you will see new things breaking as never before! Only **My Way** has all the safe guards required for success to ring out boldly at the end! Follow the **Truth I** unfold for you to find each day, then you will know your goal of endless satisfaction!

GIVE THANKS

GIVE THANKS FOR I WILL KEEP
YOUR FEET ON SOLID GROUND,
NO SINKING SAND WILL BE FOUND!
GIVE THANKS FOR HEAVEN'S HOME

CHAPTER FOURTEEN

Faith – The Truth Walk Way

When **My** children finally come to **Me** in **Truth**, then **I** release **Faith** as a constant comforter. This is as it should be for it is only by **Faith**, their own personnel **Faith**, that they truly learn to move and grow into the children of **God I** desire. Yes, **My** dear ones you must learn to **Walk** by **Faith** in all of **My Truth** as your daily habit. **Truth** flows freely from a pure heart. **My Children's** hearts are pure. Grow and learn to be obedient to **Truth** in all things, and in all of your ways.

Truth flows by and through **Love, My Love. My Love I** freely give to all who have hearts **I** give them that they use! Many children have **I** given **My Heart**, but they still are only moved by their free will. To long have **I** allowed this insult to be overlooked, but in this closing just before **Us Truth** must prevail! All things of man must be left where man desires them to be for his free will **I** honor still!

Go forward boldly, in **Faith**, knowing that **I** am with you always. **My Love** is carrying you through every trial and temptation. You should do your part and **My Love** will sustain you. *"Blessed is the man who perseveres under trial."* Tell yourself, I am strong in the Lord, and I know that **God** is supplying everything I need to do, and the things **He** wants me to. Seek the face of **Jesus** always, walk in **His** peace and experience **His Love** and **He** will see you through. *"Seek ye first the Kingdom of God and His righteousness and all these things shall be added unto you."*

The days are worthless when **I'm** ignored. See that **We** are always **Walking** close. This is a privilege not to be wasted. Listen in your heart for **My** telling words are not just for you, but they are given for you to share freely with **My Loved** ones. Stay open to this **Way**, and **Walk** daily for all is not open yet that is to be shown. Read **My Word** for growth in **My Plan** for you. Only when you are close, listening, can this phase of growth be shown.

A **Walk** into **My Purpose** is what **I'm** giving now to all and anyone who will listen with a hungry heart. Hungry hearts are opened by **Love** seeking in **Truth**. **I** am **Truth**, and **I** open the **Truth** for **My Loved** ones who will give their time listening and learning to communicate with **Me**. **All Truth** moves as **Love** calls. Only **I** can answer **Loves Call**. Seek this that **I'm** exposing in these words for they carry the life to live for **Me** that is the **True** life of eternity! Seek this with all of your time being given while in the flesh. Here is **Truth** of great worth, **Learn Love's Lessons** only **I** teach!

Go through each day confident that **God** is with you, making a way. Be an over-comer and let Faith carry you through. Step out confidently, and in joy, knowing that **God's Love** is enfolding you. Be strong in the **Lord** knowing that *"The joy of the Lord is my strength."* Put this into your mind and soul until it becomes a part of you. It will make a difference in your life. Seek to know **God's Plan** for you. Go forth boldly in the **Path He** has found for you. **Walk** in peace as **His Plan** unfolds in your life. Rest and have **Faith** in the **Lord** knowing that **His Way** is always good, and your final destination is with **Him** in **Heaven**.

This daily **Walk** on earth is becoming an earthly stroll in the heaven of **My Heart**! Never believe otherwise! **We** will see **Truth's**

Will exploding in the hearts of all those **I've** chosen to bless with **Revelation Knowledge**. This word will not be buried alone and lonely! Keep the **Truth** in all things open before you and it will become your doorway to **My Heart**. **Truth** in all things is only **My Love** opening to the full **Walk** of **My Children's** life **I** give them. The life **I** give freely is **Heaven's Walk of Love** in **My Will** and **Way**.

Only this key of **Love** accepted is the **Truth** forever to be exposed. **Eternity** is only **My Love's Truth** flowing freely where **I** desire, and it is **Exposure** to this **Life** for all who **I** waken for this blessing. **My Children** are only the exposing of **Me** in **Truth** of living. **Truth** of living is all there is or ever will be, and **I** am everything **I** desire **My Children** to be. **My** lost ones are only failure denied to live because **I** never fail!

"You shall love the Lord your God with all your heart and your neighbor as yourself." Without **Love** you are apart from **God**. **He** is **Love** and wants to bring **True Love** into your life. Having **His Love** in your heart means you are living a **Spirit-led** life and doing the will of **Jesus**. Keep the communication line open between you and the **Lord** through praise, worship and prayer. Pray that **His Will** be done in you and through you always. Fill your life with **Jesus**. The more of **Jesus** in your being means the less of self. **My Children** are to cast self aside and live for **Jesus**. Thinking only of self is living in sin. *"Be still and know that I am God."* Invite into your life the **Love, Peace** and **Joy He** has for you. Let **His Presence** cover you always and you will live in perfect peace!

My Children need **My Word** for them as they need air to breath. Feed them **Truth** for only **My Bible Truth** brings the children **I** call. Never neglect to seek **My** lost ones around you. Make this your stepping stones to **My Heart** that you **Walk** on daily. Many are called and many turn and listen, but few ever give **Me** their whole heart. Man's whole heart for me is the place, the only place, for each heart to be. **I'm** speaking now about the proper **Walk** to take to build **My Kingdom** with **Me. I'm** speaking now of the **True Walk** in the flesh. Everyone born again will be saved and come into **My Kingdom**, but **I'm** calling, a last call now, for those who seek to be more than the least!

Listen with your whole heart now, rise to the position My Heart calls you to. Love is the life, Faith is the Way, Totally is the cost! Not your will but Mine, not your Plan but My Purpose only is the Way to go!

May **God's** grace be upon you now and forever more. Live in harmony with all others as well as with **Jesus**. Know the **Word**, and stand fast in the **Word** of **God**. Abide in the **Love** of the **Lord** and **He** will give you stength. Spend quiet time with **God** and you will be strengthened as well as directed in the path that **He** has prepared for you. *"Delight thyself in the Lord and He shall give thee the the desires of thine heart."* Enjoy being in the presence of the **Lord**, take to yourself **His** glorious **Love**. Then extend to all others this **Love**. Be free through the **Holy Spirit** to **Love** others as **God** has loved you.

It is with great effort **My Children** will learn to bring themselves to **Me** in **Truth** and **Honesty**. Struggle is to be a path for many that seek a close **Walk** with **Me**. There is an enemy who **I** use to draw out and fashion the path of each and everyone **I Love. Love** does not flow freely to **My Children** for **My** weeding out of the dross is a must for perfection to abide in **My Children's** heart. Testing is sure, and overcoming is a cleansing necessary, climbing daily is the right path, and never retreating earns the **True** reward **I** give. Surely mercy and grace are forthcoming and riding on the wings of **Love. My Love** is for each overcoming child of **Mine**. Day by day **Walk** the **Way** that **I** set before you Never doubting, and always trusting, will pave your path with comfort and peace. Knowing is the trust building **I** offer when your attention is always on **Me** and **My Plan** and **Purpose** for you! Confidence building is the work of purpose bringing the wreath of victory. See **My Hand** in the works set before you and your way will be made clear. Be bold in your **Walk**, know to whom you belong, show the sureness of your desire and **I** will see you through **My Truth Only!**

"Thou will keep him in perfect peace whose mind is stayed on thee, because he trusteth in thee." Let **God's** perfect peace enfold you and the blessing of the **Lord** shall come upon you. *"Rejoice in the Lord always, again I say rejoice."* Praise **Him** constantly and receive all of the **Love He** has for you. Truly **God** inhabits the praises of **His** people. So **Walk** in **His** presence in praise. Be joyful because **He** is your loving **Heavenly Father** and **His Love** is forever! **Trust Him**, lean on **Him**, worship **Him** and live in constant companionship with the **Lord**. For **He** is your **God** and is your righteousness.

Your **Walk** is in **My Hands** when you are obedient to **My Voice**. Listen in the silence seeking to learn **My Way** each day! **Obedience** to **My Way** will become the **Path** of no return, you will not go again to your old lost way! You give your life to **Me Now** and you will become all in all for **My Father!** Yes **I** am the **Way** of your preparation for the **Father. Perfection We** ask can only come from **Perfection We** give! Learn to hear, then learn to obey, then your **Walk** will open to those **We** inspire.

This **Path** is the only sure **Way, Our Children** must be clear in their seeking. This is the only **Way We** desire. **We** do not bring false or confusing **Ways** to **Walk**. Follow the voice of **Truth** always in confidence of **True** believing! Know to whom you belong and to whom you belong will be given all of your Self never to be used again! Release of Self will become the melding into **Oneness** where your "Always" resides! Yes your **Oneness** must come to the final **Perfection!**

Still the body and allow the **Holy Spirit** within you to show the way. *"For as many as are led by the Spirit of God, they are the sons of God."* **My Children** be led by **My Holy Spirit** within you! *"The Spirit itself beareth witness with our spirit, that we are the children of God."* So being convinced that you are the child of **God**, you must take hold of the promises of **God** for your life. You must truly be led by the **Holy Spirit** and taught by the **Bible**, the **Word** of **God**. Let your mind and soul be cleansed by the Word of **God**. Diminish self as **Jesus** and **His Word** comes to live in your heart. Fill your mind with the words of **God**. Pray these words, *"Let the words of my mouth and the meditations of my heart be acceptable in thy sight, Oh, Lord my strength and my redeemer."*

The days vanish before you and where are you going? Learn while **I** am still calling you, listen and hear **My Voice** in your heart. Only with **Me** will you ever find pleasure for evermore. You are **My Child Now** and yet you say you don't know where you are going? If you really knew, how will that change you right Now? You are on a trip that goes on forever, and the end is still in your hands. Flee as you will right now, to where would you go?

The only reasonable thing is to do the things **I've** told you in the **Bible**. You will never be in full charge of where you are going only in **My** arms can you find your **True Path**. Learn to listen and obey, then believe you're on **My Way** for you. This is your **Walk** of **Trust** and **My** challenge to draw you. You right **Now** will **Walk** a **Walk** of **Loving Trust** or **Walk** on in questioning fear. Choose **Loving Trust!**

Live a life covered by the **Presence** of **God**. Deposit the **Word** into your heart and soul. Be led by the **Holy Spirit** always in such a manner that you will ward off the evil that would tear you down. Be in prayer constantly, praising, worshiping, and interceding for others. Have a heart full of thanksgiving as you remember all the blessings the **Lord** has showered upon you, and clear your mind of negative thoughts. Do not have a critical nature but find the good in all. Open your soul so **God** can do a work through you. **Love** is the answer! **Let His Love** change you into a loving child of **God**. **His Love** is all powerful and will work wonders in your life.

The recording daily of these words **I** give are to be kept for referral and study for the children. Do with them as **I** instruct. This is to be a record also of the expanding **Truth** in the last days. Don't think this is strange, am **I** not with you? **Truth** must become more apparent; how else will the children be sure? More care should be given to **Truth** in **My Words** than is being shown around the world. Every preacher does not speak all of **My Truth** nor do many even search for it; they just are led by each other not **Me**! **Truth** exposed is where **True Hope** is reposed! Only following the whole of **Truth** brings the children home! This is just a record of **My Desires** so mark it as **My Purpose** revealed in **Truth** for these **End Times**!

You need **My Strength**, and **My Power** in your life. Remember to lean on **Me**. Depend on **Me** for all things. You are **My** children and **I** have many blessings for you but you must learn to receive. Receive into your life the blessings of the **Holy Spirit**. Know and have faith in your **God** who **Loves** you, who created you to be **His Family**. Deposit **My Word** and **My Promises** into your heart that they may become a part of you, then when you need answers from **Me** you will have them from the **Word**.

Release the teachings and guidance from the **Holy Spirit**. Let **Him Truly** be your comforter and **your** helper, for that is **His** purpose in your life. **Walk** always in **God's** Presence. Let **His Peace, Love,** and **Joy** saturate **your** being and change you into the child of **God He** created you to be.

Make each day the time of **Our Togetherness** and **I** can make each day **Our Walk** in **Love**! **I** must leave this choosing of occasion up to you so you hold **Our Oneness Walk** in your hands! Keep this note always before you; never come to the place that you ask **Me** why **I** didn't do this or that for you! **Truly Our Walk** in **Togetherness** is basically just how you allow **Me time** with you! **We** are **Now One** but the growth of **Our Oneness** is **Now** in your hands. There is to come that **time** when transfer must be made! Dwell, think on, and consider that which **I** have just set before you! When will your **Walk** become **Our Walk**, and then **My Walk**? **Spiritual** growth is ongoing, when will your **Walk** grow from self led to your Spirit **Led**, to **Our Togetherness Walk**, and finally to **Our Total Oneness** of **Together Walk** where **All** is of **The Father**?

Rest in **Me**, and be confident that all things will be added unto you as needed. **I** know your thoughts, your cares and worries, that is why **I** implored you to *"Cast your cares upon me for I careth for you." You must trust in the **Lord** for all things at all times. "His yoke is easy and His burden is light."* **Walk** in and remain in **His Will** and all things will work together for good. Search yourself often to be sure that you are in **His Will**. **Walk** in the peace that comes when you know and are in **His Will**. **His Walk** is free from care, **His Will** lifts you up and over the problems of the day. Be an over-comer through **Him**!

When **Our** time moves as **I** desire it to then **We** will have attained the **Oneness** of **Perfection** which is the **Forever Walk**. Keep ever drawing your self out and drawing more of **Me** in every day. Don't ask how, just learn by attempting to do! **I** am always with you to help; just ask! **Walking** properly is learning daily to **Walk** as **I** require. Believe to achieve, in trying is growing! Your **Walk** continues so never grow weary, just grow closer and **I** will give you rest.

All **I** say and all you do is what brings you through. Only together with **Us** is the **Walk I** call for. **I** never set unattainable goals, see that you also never set or seek them. All things work together when you keep **Our** closeness real! **Believing** trust is your daily **Walk**; it's made easier when you know **I'm** always there. I hesitate to move in haste and you will find the best place by similar caution exercised. Wait upon **Me** more, then you will surely know your way.

Keep every day the day **I Walk** with you, and then **We** will see clearly the path of **Truth** unfolding. Yes **Truth** will unfold properly as you keep your desire growing to **Walk My Way** each day, not once in a while but hour by hour until it becomes moment by moment! You may say why, but soon you will be so close **My Truth** will fill your time as air fills your home! Only children who **Walk** this close become the ones that allow **Love** to grow as **I** desire. For all **My Desire** for more children coming into **My Plan** is only fulfilling **My Love's Desire** to expand and grow toward ever increasing expansion!

Try to see **Love** as a vapor expanding touching everything **I** create. All **Creation** reacts as **Love** is outreaching into **My Sea of Nothing**. Flowers are a good example of this absorption **I'm** trying to explain. They can exhibit beauty of color, and they can sing with the harmony of **Love**. They can wave and show forth the perfume of **Love** in many ways. Only **Love** expressed, freely opens all creation to show forth part of **Myself! My Children** only openly show **Me** properly when **Love** is more apparent than self. Open your heart to **Love's Truth** and your **Walk** will become a flower strewn way!

Yes, **I** will go before you, and your path is prepared by **Me**. **Walk** it in peace for **I** am with you! Just as **I** had to **Walk** in the flesh all **My Loved Ones** will **Walk** their **Walk**. Make each day a **Walk** fulfilling **My Purpose** for you, and **I** am with you **always**. Keep your eyes upon **Me** and **My Way**, for **I** will bless and keep you! Find joy even when the circumstances are difficult. Rise above the things of the world and seek the face of **Jesus**. Give praise always to a loving **God** who is watching over you. Let everything you are going through be a lesson in over-coming, a lesson in **Spritual** growth.

There are many doors for men to open in each life, but there is only **One Door** that counts! Find that door, search with all of your heart, **Open** that door and **know** it's this one to go through. Seek and you shall find when you search with a **True Heart** and a **True Goal!** The **True Heart** searches for **Truth** nothing else matters, find **Truth** above all things. **Truth** in life, **Truth** in living, **Truth** that satisfies! Only **Truth**, as your **Heart Search** carries you, will be your **Walk** that satisfies. **Heart Desires** make True steps flow in Love. **Head Desires** lead to error and death. **Heart Desires** inspires, leading to **Me**. Only the **Heart Search** for **Love** brings **Head Desires** of great **Worth**. **I Am LOVE!**

You have accepted **Jesus** in your heart therefore you are a child of **God**. **Walk** as one who is led by the **Holy Spirit** for this is **God's** way for you. Receive and release into your life the promises and blessings **God** has for you. Bring forth into your being the fruit of the **Holy Spirit**, these blessings from the **Lord** are yours. Live constantly in **His Love**, let peace fill your soul. Do not be crushed by the Worlds problems, but be an over-comer. Lean on the **Lord** for **He** cares for you, and **He** is your protector and provider. Remember, *"He which hath begun a good work in you will perform it until the day of Jesus Christ."*

The ones who are willingly drawing closer to **Me**, even in this last short time, have touched **My Heart** in such a meaningful **Way**. **I** send all **Truth** and when it is so ignored **I** seek to move on and close this time. But just for those few dear ones whose hearts awaken seeking **Me**, **I** am stretching their time to grow. Let your time be spent for **Me** now and you will know **Me** as few others ever will. Come **listen** in your heart, for **Truth** flowing opens the inner gates of **Heaven** making a way **I** desire for you to **Walk!**

Only **True Truth Seekers** are **Walking** the **Way** of **Truth Now!** This is time spent that **Truly** paves your streets with **Gold!** All streets of **Mine** are not **Gold**, some are still hard trails of learning in **My Loving Way! Heaven** is **Truly** a variety pack of learning **Love's Ways.** All who enter **Heaven** will find a growing time of **Love.** All children enter this growing **Way of Truth** unfolding with lessons of **Love** their daily food. **I'm** telling this now so some who read it will grow in their last flesh time to know **Love's Truth** and great worth being given **Now!**

Lean on **Me** and **My Strength** shall be your strength. Remember, *"The joy of the Lord is my strength."* **I** give to you all things that are necessary for this **Walk.** Be bold, going forward and **I** will make a way for you. Hear **My Word** today, be a blessing in showing **Love** to **My Children** by loving them as **I** have loved you. Be kind, gentle and patient for **I** have put these blessings in your heart through the **Holy Spirit.** Show forth the character of **Jesus.** Prepare yourselves for **My Kingdom** in meekness and self control and **I** will lift you up!

These days may seem endless but **I** assure you there is an end **coming!** It will be time spent **Now** that builds the place where you shall stand then! Hear these words of **My Truth** and act accordingly. Only those who hear **My Voice**, and in hearing become **Doers** of **Truth**, can **I** save and hold as **True Children of Mine.** Here is **Truth Worth Telling** to children who have hearts to **Hear, Listen and Do!**

Then who shall I call, who can be told these **Truths**? Who will listen with a **True Heart** and **Purpose**? Only those who listen to **Me** will know in their hearts that this is work of **My Spirit** not of **My** children! **My True Ones** will become what their own choice has made them. **I'll** keep teaching **My Truth's** to those **I** can reach and **We** will grow close and closer!

Be faithul in the **Lord**. Rise up and be strong for **I** am blessing you. As you rest in **Me** your strength will return. Therefore lean on **Me** for **I** care for you and **I** am your strength. Have a thankful heart, full of praise and worship keeping your eyes on **Jesus**. *"Thy will be done in me and through me, oh lord, my strength and my redeemer."* Pray for others constantly for **I** hear your prayers and answer them. Be joyful in the **Lord** for you are in **My Will**. Let the **Holy Spirit** lead you always for this is **My Will**. Be lifted up through the power of the fruit of the **Spirit.** These blessings are yours and will help you accomplish **My Will** for your life. Flow in the **Spirit**, let go and let **God** lead you in all ways!

It's good to review **Our Writing**, just try to remember all of this that **We** are doing is **truly** building a future so don't let the past drag you down. **My** timing is always confusing to **My Children** only because they don't yet **Walk** in the **Spirit**! Keep your place and position always clear in mind. **Our Walk** is a climb into a place you still know little about! **Earth Truths** have only some resemblance to **Spirit Truths**. Your patience is required now in this area.

Growing Spiritually will surprise many by how long it takes some to navigate successfully! Lean more on **Me** and be open to **Truth** flowing freely to and through you. You are **My** companions and **I** am **Walking** this **Walk** with you, and in you, but not for you, you must **Walk** it as the **Father** releases it. Let this knowledge be a true comfort to you for it is displaying the surety of your **Walk**!

The **Way** of the **Lord** is good. Follow in **His** footsteps always. Be the child of **God** you were created to be. Live in a state of peace for **His Presence** is your covering. Lift up your soul and heart above and beyond the cares of the world and into **His** realm of righteousness. Let **His Leading** show the **Way**. Listen carefully for **His** still soft voice and it will become a **knowing** within. **Truth** is what you receive from the **Father.** Live by it. Praise and **Worship Him** and live in the fullness of **His Presence**. **Walk** confidently knowing **He** is with you. Keep always a thankfu heart with praise on your lips for *"God inhabits the praises of his people."*

This day is a good time to receive all of the blessings **I've** stored up for you. Open your heart and let your mind receive all **I've** planned and released. Milestones and cornerstones all have a place in **Our Time** of growing. Some things are worth knowing because **"believing"** in **Truth, My Truth,** is the stepping stone for **True Children** of **Mine** to use. **The Walk** in **Love I Desire** for all of **My Children** does have special times and special places of great growth. These changes that are from **Me** come to each one more as **I Desire** than from **One Great Move of Mine** at some single time. These kinds of great moves involving everybody **I've** carefully recorded in **My Bible.** Special moves outside of what is scripturally said seldom happens. Man's imaginations run away with him in the heat of his own frenzy. **Walk** your **Walk** with **Me** as **I** lead you personally for the **True Blessings** that last forever!

Proclaim the **Word of God. Speak His Promises** to you, let your mouth speak and your ears hear what **God** has promised to you. Claim your inheritances in the **Lord. Miracles** happened when the **Lord** spoke. Use words, positive words, as weapons of warfare. Combat the enemy by the words of your mouth. Take the **God-Given Authority** over evil by claiming what is yours, by speaking **God's Words, His Promises** to you. Let your faith grow. Believe that which the **Lord** says is **Truth** and a positive force. *"For I am the lord that healeth thee." "But my god shall supply all your need according to his riches in glory by Christ Jesus." "I have come that they might have life and that they might have it more abundantly."* **God** is faithful to **His Word,** it is **His** promise to you!

As days flee away, the works of **My Desire** shall increase, see that the importance of this time is not missed! Men are still as of old seeking but not willing to go far or look very deep. The expansion of **My Plans** wither at man's lack of drive or eagerness to pursue the **Truth I** hold out as worth. Do not copy such foolishness. The purpose and desires of **My Heart** are to become a clear path of learning, growing, and spreading **Truth.** Correcting the errors of teaching falls short of fulfilling **My Desires** for **Truth** in all things. **Only Truth** pursuit brings anyone to their **True Place** with **Me.** Open up **My Bible** in all **Truth** as it should be stated. **Truth** should be clearly expressing the words that bring **My Orders** and **Way** in clarity! **Truth** brings only peace and contentment not contention and upset!

Allow the **Holy Spirit** to work through you. Make yourself available, be that empty earthen vessel that **He** can use. There may be cracks and flaws in your vessel but **His Light** will shine through. **He** will build you up while shining **His Light** through you so others may know **God. He** does not require perfection but availability. As you let go and let **God He** is able to bring you from **Glory to Glory. He** will lift you up to heavenly places for you are joint-heirs with **Jesus.** In **Peace** and **Love** go forth each day confident that Jesus is with you, and that **He** will make a way to use you for **His Glory.**

FELLOWSHIP

LET OUR FELLOWSHIP FLOW,
SEEK NO OTHER PLAN,
OR WAY TO WALK OR GO.

LET OUR FELLOWSHIP BE YOUR ALL,
SEEK NO OTHER PLAN,
THEN YOU'LL NEVER FALL.

LET OUR FELLOWSHIP SHOW LOVE,
SEEK NO OTHER PLAN,
IT WILL BE SENT FROM ABOVE.

CHAPTER FIFTEEN

Just a Closer Look

The desires of **My Heart** are to see **My Children** profit from all of **My Words** that **I** give them corporately and individually. **I** never skimp or hold back from **My True Truth Seekers**, and **I** give freely to the rest of **My** children as they open their hearts seeking. **My Truth** is so necessary for their Physical and Spiritual growth; but when they seek just a little, or only what they think they need, then **My** wonderful blessings fall far short for them and **My Word** seems to go wanting.

Come now these are the very last days for the entire **Bride,** and so many are going to wake up to great surprises. The tale of **My Sea of Nothing** is an **End of Age** blessing to those whose hearts are true and their searching fruitful. To the listening, obedient ones come wonderful blessings upon blessings that delight and excite them! Search this work here presented and find new **Truths** of your close, and very far away blessings.

This chapter will take a close look at the Scriptures to see what **I** say about your **Focus** and where it should be. If **My Words** have been fully supported by you this should only be an exercise in where you have been, and where are now! **My** teachings should have brought your walk to the same place **Jesus** was when **He** had **His** walk in the flesh. **I** change not, **I** am the same yesterday, today, and forever, so this teaching should be a stroll over the same path

Jesus walked. To set **My** goal before you at the start **I'll** make this lesson easy. **I** desire that every child of **Mine** could wind up their time in the flesh by saying "I finally came to the place that I do nothing but what the **Father** tells me to do." **I** will right here give the short quick picture of the walk **I** desire each child to walk.

After your born-again experience receive the "Water Baptism" with its sealing into **My** resurretion blessing **I** intend for you. **My** goal then would be for you to come out of the water receiving the **Baptism** in the **Holy Spirit** speaking in tongues. Now you have the **Spiritual** tools to read and study **My Word [Bible]**. Learn to grow in the **Word** led by **My Holy Spirit**. This soon should lead you to hear from and learn to walk and talk with **Jesus**. As self is "Put Down" then covered up, then put out; **I** will come and sup with you and **We** will walk, talk, and fellowship in the **Spirit** together until you, as **Jesus** did, can say, "I'll now do nothing but what **The Father** tells me." WHAT DO YOU NOW IMAGINE YOUR FOCUS SHOULD BE?

SEEKING MY GOALS

In these very last days **I** am crying out to **My** obedient children to come to **Me** as never before believing to hear **My** voice, obey **My** voice, and come to **The Father**. [Finally as your **Father** who reigns forevermore] In this manner **I** am able to find out the children best suited for quality and important positions as **Jesus' Bride**. As **My Word** has taught, **His Bride** will live in the **Heavenly Jerusalem** and satellite the **Earth**. They will be living in the **Space** of the **Universe** from where their life of forever will begin. They will be set up as **God's Kings** and **Priests** forever; this is only a beginning, and where they go from there on is still to be revealed! But know this; **I** will begin to choose from those while they are still growing in the flesh. This is why it is so important for their compliance now in these last very few days!

The answer is in The Word the only place to begin!

The following is a list of scriptures showing clearly the **Father's Heart's** desire by **His** call going out to all the children in **His Family** since Moses first headed the Nation Israel until the end time of Revelation Chapter 3. **Read and carefully study** how **God** asks time and time again for **His Children to Hear, Heed, Listen and Obey!** Listen to the **Holy Spirit, Jesus**, and **The Father. The Father** personally wants to teach each one; *John 6:45* as an example. There are many more scriptures that say the same or similarly, but the following words say it clearly!

Deut. 4:29,30,36; 5:26,27; 8:3,20; 29:29; 30:8,10,14,17,20; 1Sam. 3:1,3,4,6,8,10; 1Kings 19:9,12,13; Ps. 25:14; 29:3-5,7-9; 32:8; 34:11; 46:10; 50:7; 73:24; 91:15; 95:7; 107:11; 143:8,10; Prov. 1:23,33; 2:1-6; 5:1,7; 8:4-8; 16:9; 20:12; 23:19; 25:2; Isa. 30:30; 42:9,23; 48:8; 50:5; 54:13; 55:1-3;11; Jer. 30:2; 38:20; 42:3,21; Ezek. 33:10; 44:5; Dan.2:28; Hos. 4:1,6; Matt. 4:4; 7:24; 11:15; 13:23; Mark 4:9; 9:7; John 5:19-24,30,37,38; 6:45,63; 7:38,39; 8:31,32,47; 10:3,4,16,27; 12:50; 14:23,24-26; 16:13; 17:8; 18:37; 1 Cor. 2:10; 3:20; 4:5; 6:17; 14:5,6; 11Cor. 13:3; Gal. 1:12; Eph. 4:21; Col.3:16; Heb. 1:2; 2:3; 3:7,15; 4:7,12; 12:25; 11 Pet. 1:17,18,21; Rev. 2:7,11,17,29; 3:6,13,20,22.

STUDY IN QUIETNESS

Why should you try to find more and more of **Jesus**, or **God**? Simply because **He** is calling you, and your **Love of Jesus** compels you to seek and keep on seeking. David says in *Psalm 16:11, "Thou wilt show me the path of life: in thy presence is fullness of joy; at thy right hand there are pleasures for evermore."* Also He says in the following Psalms: *Psalm 40:8, "I delight to do thy will, O my*

God: yea, thy law is within my heart." and *Psalm 73:25, "Whom have I in heaven but thee? And there is none upon earth that I desire besides thee." Psalm 46:10, "Be still, and know that I am God: I will be exalted among the heathen, I will be exalted on earth." Psalm 63:1,2, "O God, thou art my God; early will I seek thee: my soul thirsteth for thee, my flesh longest for thee in a dry and thirsty land, where no water is."* Peter says in *1 Peter 1:8, "Whom having not seen, ye love; in whom, though now you see him not, yet believing, ye rejoice with joy unspeakable and full of glory."* And this is an appealing call from God Himself: *St. Matthew 11:28, "Come unto me, all ye that labor and are heavy laden, and I will give you rest."*

Where else in the Scriptures do you find some good examples?

Noah, in *Genesis 6:9; "These are the generations of Noah: Noah was a just man and perfect in his generations, and Noah walked with God."* And in *Genesis 6:22, "Thus did Noah; according to all that God commanded him, so did he."*

Elijah, If He wasn't listening He wouldn't have heard the still small voice, *I Kings 19:11-13.*

Moses, He is probably the finest example in so many places in the Bible! You find the scriptures that support his walk!

Habakkuk, *Chapter 2:1,2, "I will stand upon my watch, and set me upon the tower, and will watch to see what he will say unto me, and what I shall answer when I am reproved. And the Lord answered me, and said, Write the vision, and make it plain upon the tables, that he may run that readeth it."* This clearly shows that Habakkuk was in a regular conversation with the **Father** and he wrote what the **Lord** said to him.

There are scriptures that suggest you rise early in the morning and find a quiet place to meet with the **Lord**. The time and place is your choice, but find a place where you can be physically and mentally refreshed. How long you stay there is your choice, **God** is always there for you. How much do you want **His** word and/or desire it? Your days are numbered so apply your heart to what you are doing. *Psalm 90:12, "So teach us to number our days, that we may apply our hearts unto wisdom."*

In this quiet time seek to be still and just listen, you are sitting and waiting on the **Lord.** This is a time when you can grow in the **Spirit** and nothing apparent will seem to be happening. Just listen and dwell on nothing, just listening! Can you believe for this? [This is when **The Father** will build you up **Spiritually**] There are many other things you can do: Prayer in devotions, **Bible** reading, silent communion, and worship. Sing to the **Lord** in your understanding and sing in the **Spirit**. Some want to just pray, love **Jesus**, quote the word, and sense **His** presence in the silence. **My** dear children **I** have opened **My Heart** to you and poured **My Love** out in all of these words, surely something has touched your heart. Come to **Me** and be **My Bride** Forever!

I DESIRE TO BRING A BLESSING IN CLOSING, *Isaiah 57:15, "For thus saith the high and lofty One that inhabiteth eternity, whose name is Holy; I dwell in the high and holy place, with him also the is of a contrite and humble spirit, and to revive the spirit of the humble, and to revive the heart of the contrite ones."* In **My Word I** have revealed a hint of **Truth** to be picked up by **My** obedient listening ones. Yes, **I** do inhabit eternity fore in **My S.O.N. All** exists, all of **My** past, it's never lost and all of **My** children are present with all of **Our Everlasting life** yet to come. That is what is meant when **I** say with him also that is of a contrite and humble spirit. Can you grasp this that **I** am saying? **I** speak only what is true to **My** listening children. **I** intend for this tale of **My S.O N.** to stir and awaken hearts to **My Eternal Existence** and give to them a glimise of the What, When, and Where of it. Now can you better bellieve and understand something of why **I** call **My Own Place** by the title of **Sea Of Nothing?**

Only to **My** growing, listening, children do **I** give this privilege. To just say this much shows clearly, when you give it some depth of thought, why **I** can not explain much of any of this place. **I** said before in **My Prologue**, where **I** call it **My S.O.N**, there is nothing **I** want to tell about it in any detail because man, while in the flesh, has little or no capacity to comprehend its size, scope, or to ever begin to understand its purpose. How can **I** have all **Eternity** held before **Me** at once? How can **I** see, live in and know all that ever has been and all that ever will be? Is this not **True**? Could any child ever have that relationship with **All Future, Present, and Past**? The how of **My Place** can not be **explained**, and **I** will not do so until in some far future of **Our Walk** when **My** close ones are much more like **Jesus**!

This future place, as **I** have already said, **Jesus** or the **Angels** are seldom invited to enter, only when **I** require support they can properly execute. Explanation now is not useful and would serve no more purpose than that which this book is disclosing. It is **My** desire to be fulfilled as **I** seek to open some futher **Hope** of a **FAR FUTURE**, and give insight into **My Children's Future Inheritance**. **Truth** is **Jesus** and **Truth** is for all **My** dear ones, only as they are properly equiped to make that **Truth** useful. *I Kings 8:60, "That all of the people of the earth may know that the Lord is God, and there is none else."*

There will come a time at the end that **All** people of the earth will know that the **Lord** is **God**, but **I** desire **My Son's Bride** to be the first to know these kinds of **Truth** early, only because **I Love Them** and they **Love Me**! It is because of this **Love** that release is given for them to have this simple insight into **My True Place of Always**.

Psalm 39:4, "Lord, make me to know my end, and the measure of my days,what it is; that I may know how frail I am." **My Children** have made similar pleas throughout all their ages, but **I** will wait no more because the **Bride** is standing at the door of **Forever**, and **I** desire to release this kind of encouraging answer for their comfort before they enter their next plase.

Psalm 46:10 "Be still, and know that I am God: I will be exalted among the heathen, I will be exalted in the earth." In the **Bride** many have been obedient to this call of **Mine**, but especially in these last days. **I** release this encouraging messege that they will be blessed.

Psalm 100:3, "Know ye that the Lord he is God: it is he that hath made us, and not we ourselves; we are his people, the sheep of his pasture." **I** desire to release this story to fill **My** desire to reward the children [**The Bride of Christ**] at this time. They have little time left before they will walk in the Spirit just as **Jesus** does today. Is it not proper to bless them a little while it is their last time in their flesh walk?

Proverbs 22:20,21 "Have I not written to thee excellent things in counsels and knowledge, That I might make thee know the certainty of the words of truth; that thou mightest answer the words of truth to them that send into thee?" This book then is **My** follow-on bringing futher words of **Truth** to support, aid and direct you carefully into **ALL** **I** have to reveal. **I** am building in **My** dear listening ones an ability to recognize and be blesssed with **My Truth** unfolding. Let this **Truth** set well in your understanding that **I** may be able to **Truly** call you **My Children**, yet to be much more!

EVER GROWING LOVE

LET THIS BE THE END OF DAZE,

COME TO ME I'LL LIFT THE HAZE.

IN MY LOVE YOU'LL DRAW MY PEACE,

IN HEAVEN'S REALM STRIFE WILL CEASE.

IN MY ARMS YOU'LL FIND YOUR PLACE.

IN MY ARMS YOU'LL END THE RACE.

YES IN MY LOVE FOREVERMORE,

YOU'VE LANDED ON FUTURE'S SHORE.